MAKING WAVES

By Kenneth Pearce

Signature Books

Published by
Signature Books
3945 Opal Street
Oakland, CA 94609, USA
(415) 932-7078

Printed in the United States of America.

Library of Congress Cataloging-in-Publication Data

Pearce, Kenneth, 1931–
    Making waves.

    I. Title.
PS3566.E214M3   1987   813'.54   87-4606
ISBN 0-941503-28-3

NOTE FROM THE AUTHOR

This book is a dramatized account of some of the wild and frantic experiences I enjoyed while serving as ship's hairdresser aboard a series of luxury liners for a five-year period during the mid-Fifties.

However, in order to protect the guilty from those who might have thought they were purely innocent at the time, I have fashioned these adventures into a novel that, hopefully, will be as much fun for the readers as it was for me and my colleagues while it was happening.

The result is a combined factual and fictionalized composite of events in which all the names have been changed. In this way, we've managed to have fun at everybody's expense without offending anyone, least of all the readers who, we hope, will derive the most benefit from the rather "freestyle" manner in which we have played with the facts.

Kenneth Pearce

ONE

As a rather quiet little boy growing up in middle-class London, Paul Barrington took it for granted that his compulsive urge to travel and see the world would never become a reality. In school, his favorite subject had been art, with geography running a close second. However, when it came to such boring gibberish as algebra or geometry, he drew a total blank.

At the age of 14, it was his talent as a sketch artist, rather than his yen to travel, that led to his choice of a career. He began serving a four-year apprenticeship as a barber and hairstylist. He had to put his urge to see the world on hold while he spent those years learning his craft. Whenever he had the time to think about it, however, he feared there wouldn't be much call for oceangoing hairdressers.

Happily, there was one big consolation in being forced to stifle his longing for faraway places: he liked working as a hairdresser, partly because it fulfilled his artistic needs — Paul could draw before he could read or write — and also because he loved being around women. Not for the reasons most people might assume in the gaily liberated Eighties. Indeed, all during his apprenticeship in the Forties, Paul couldn't remember meeting a single "gay" hairdresser. There were a lot of jolly ones, of course; but as for gays, perhaps in those days they remained so discreetly in the closet that no one took much notice when they came out. In any case, from an early age Paul Barrington knew exactly *why* he liked girls, and it had nothing to do with borrowing their clothes.

While it was true that his education as a hairstylist began at the tender age of 14, his native curiosity about females had gotten underway much earlier, at the age of 11. But, since he initially thought he was the only little boy in the world who harbored such desires, he didn't have the nerve to do anything about it until he was 13. It was then, while he was doing some practice hairstyling on the unruly mop of a girl from down the block, that he first learned what that sort of propinquity did to his vitals. Almost overnight, he discovered what it meant to be a good neighbor and how it helped when the girl in question knew a little something about hospitality.

True, not all the clients he worked on in the future would lead Paul to dreams of romantic conquest. In some of the more extreme cases, where perhaps some bulbous dowager demanded to look like Rita Hayworth, Paul viewed his career as more of a challenge than an aphrodisiac.

Apart from Paul's on-the-job apprenticeship, he also trained with a well-known genius in the field of hairstyling, a Professor Belmont. He studied with the professor every Thursday afternoon, on his one day off each week. In this way, he learned many invaluable tricks of the trade, so, by the time he was ready to turn professional, he felt a lot more seasoned and knowledgeable than many of his peers.

He completed his four-year apprenticeship in 1949 and was immediately drafted into the RAF. He was 18 years old and certain that his childhood dreams of travel would at last come true. He volunteered for overseas duty, eager to get his wings and fly off to the far corners of the world. But this didn't happen. He was stationed in Northern England during the entire two-year hitch. As it turned out, only those men who had voluntarily enlisted in the service were given travel opportunities. RAF draftees were not so lucky. Paul never saw a plane and never got off the ground.

Frustrated and bored by the daily routine, he more than made up for it during his weekend forays into the realm of sweetness and romance. By now, Paul had grown tall, lithe, and handsome, the kind of sensitive yet rugged guy to whom most women felt easily drawn. At 18, he was six feet tall, slim and broad-shouldered with wavy blond hair, wide-set blue eyes, high cheekbones and a full yet delicately boyish mouth. When it first occurred to Paul that women liked the way he looked, he was genuinely delighted. Women were the creatures he most wanted to please in life, so wasn't it fortunate that he pleased them so visibly, even before he'd had the chance to do something he knew would please them more?

It was during that two-year hitch in the RAF that Paul learned to play the field, when it came to such things as romance and girls and erotic calisthenics. He was far away from home and family, as well as some of the teenaged cuties he had dated while attending school; now all he had to break the military monotony of his weekends was a carousel of willing local playmates. If his four-year apprenticeship had trained him for his craft, those two years of promiscuous weekends fully rounded out his education in the arena of lovemaking.

At the time, he made all sorts of intriguing discoveries. Women loved the way he worshiped their bodies in bed, with a kind of sensual reverence. From the beginning, Paul's need for affection was uppermost in his relationships with women, so he was tender instead of rough, his caresses slow and languid instead of rushed or selfishly demanding. He could be both sweet and fiercely virile all in the same mad, tumbling hour of passion, and he learned very quickly that women wanted a soft and sensual time of sharing, not some savage, bestial coupling.

As for forming lasting attachments, Paul kept strictly to the serviceman's motto: "When not near the girl you love, you'd bloody well manage to love the girl you're near." In short, in those days his best girl was usually the one who was close enough to reach for in his hour of need.

Not that he broke any hearts, mind you, for he told no lies and made no false promises. Whenever they asked if they would see him again, he'd give them a jaunty grin and say, "You never know what the future might bring." Privately, he knew he was much too young to be using the word "forever," no matter which warm body he was embracing at the moment.

Paul was 20 when he got out of the RAF in 1951, and he had no trouble finding a job in a reputable West End salon. He rented a cozy little flat of his own nearby, having decided he would no longer be content to live at home with his well-meaning mum and dad and his older sister. Of course, his mother was a fabulous cook, so he never missed visiting the family for Sunday dinners.

It wasn't until years later, when Paul was living and working in the States, that he realized how surprisingly little stigma was involved if you were a man living in London some 30 years ago and you chose to be a hairdresser. Certainly it didn't occur to any member of his family to feel embarrassed that he had chosen what might be termed an unmanly occupation. For one thing, truly accomplished hairstylists earned good wages and, in his field, Paul had fast become the sort of artist who was in short supply. He had that special flair, an extra *panache* that many others lacked, even those who were more proficient technically than he. And he knew instinctively what women wanted, too, whether it involved simple charm and charisma, or more personal modes of attention after the close of business. In some cases, a little action above and beyond the call of duty kept his clients coming back for more than just a wash and a set. Because his parents were practical people, they had the good sense to be proud of his success, knowing he had chosen a craft that would offer him a lifetime of job security.

Paul had been working at his new job only a few months when his old friend and mentor, Professor Belmont, visited him at the shop and invited him for lunch, and made him a surprising offer.

When they were settled at a table, the professor first reminded Paul how upset he had been that Paul had never been given the opportunity to travel while in the Service.

"You remember, Paul?"

"Of course I remember. But there's not much I can do about that now, Professor — I'm trapped in my job here in London."

"But you don't have to be trapped, dear boy. That's what I'm trying to tell you. I've a very good friend who runs the hairstyling salons and shops aboard luxury liners. You know, the kind of big, sumptuous vessels that take those long cruises all over the world." Paul stared at him. "You mean it's possible to do what I do on board a ship?"

"But of course it is, Paul. You didn't know that? Sometimes those vessels are out to sea for as long as 90 days, and the people who can afford passage require every service they're used to on land, including doctors and cooks and stewards and maids. And since we're talking about a lot of floating glamour here, what the women passengers really want is the tender loving care they can only get from their hairdresser."

Paul grew so excited by this idea, he could hardly choke down his food when it was brought to him. "Tender loving care on a luxury liner," he muttered giddily. "My God, it sounds too good to be true. Tell me, when do I shove off?"

"Now, wait a minute," Belmont laughed. "You'd best save some of that exuberance for later. This isn't the sort of choice they make overnight. First, you must have an interview, then a medical exam. But, because I've given you the highest recommendation, I'm sure they'll dispense with the bother of testing your hairdressing skills." He reached into his pocket and pulled out a business card. "You go to this address on your first afternoon off," he said, handing Paul the card, "and just mention my name."

"Oh, Professor! I don't know how to thank you. I'm going around the world, and it's all paid for." He eyed Belmont warily. "They *do* pay my way, don't they?"

"Of course they do. That goes without saying."

Paul grinned, his head spinning with a world of far-flung fantasies and possibilities. Then he looked worried again. "I've never been to sea before, you know. What do I do if I get seasick?"

The professor smiled. "You try your damnedest not to throw up on a customer."

Paul laughed wildly at that. "Oh, well, if it happens, I'll just say, 'But didn't you know, Lady Plushmouth? Vomit shampoo is all the rage this season!' "

When he thought about this later, Paul realized that it wouldn't be all that funny if it turned out he was unable to function at sea. There was also the problem of maintaining his balance while creating an intricate hairstyle. He had an idea the salon chair might be fastened to the floor, but he feared that wouldn't be much help if he tilted to the lee side with a pair of scissors in his hands, especially if he landed in Lady Plushmouth's lap while wielding that lethal weapon. He decided to confront those obstacles one at a time.

On the following Thursday afternoon, Paul went to the London offices of the P&O Shipping Line for his interview. There he was also given his medical exam, which he passed with flying colors.

"Congratulations, Mr. Barrington," said the executive who had interviewed him, a man by the name of Hiram Wilson. "You have been chosen to join the hairstyling staff of one of our newest liners, the *Chusan*."

"Marvelous!" Paul beamed at him. "Shall I go home and pack? Of course, I'll have to give some sort of notice at the shop . . . they've been very decent to me. . ." He stopped talking when he saw the frown on Wilson's face. "What is it, sir? Have I said something wrong?"

"No, Mr. Barrington. It's just that there's a slight misunderstanding here. The opening we have in mind for you won't be available for four months."

"Four months?" Paul gasped. "Oh, no . . . I had no idea!"

"I'm sorry, I thought Professor Belmont would have told you."

Paul sighed. "Well, sir, he did say I should save my exuberance for later. But he didn't say how much later."

Wilson gave him a crisp smile of dismissal. "Actually, you're rather lucky. Some of these assignments are booked as much as eight or nine months in advance."

"Lord, it's a little like being pregnant, isn't it?"

With that, Wilson's smile faded. "Good day, Mr. Barrington. We'll be in touch."

That night, Paul felt very low and disconsolate. He phoned one of his new crop of girl friends and took her out to a movie. But he was so depressed and distracted, he all but missed his target when he bent over to kiss her goodnight.

"You've been thinking of another girl all night long," she complained. "How dare you try to use me to forget someone else? Who is she?"

"*Chusan,*" Paul muttered, "and I hear she's beautiful. If only I could get a closer look at her."

"Chusan?" The girl was livid. "You mean you're in love with some Oriental-type person and I'm your second choice?"

"Oh, no, you've got it all wrong."

7

"Don't lie to me!" She slapped his face and ran into the house.

Paul couldn't sleep that night. After being primed for instant adventure on the high seas, he'd had all the wind knocked out of his sails with the utterance of just two words: "four months."

TWO

During the next day or two, Paul kept thinking of those four months as if they were a prison term. But, one night later that week, he received a surprise phone call at home that told him he might be getting some time off for good behavior.

It was the P&O executive, Mr. Wilson.

"Mr. Barrington, there's been a sort of emergency."

Paul's heart sank. "You mean you've changed your mind?"

"No, of course not. But we *have* changed the date. One of our chief hairstylists was suddenly taken ill last night, and we need an expert replacement fast."

"How fast?" Paul asked, his spirits soaring.

"The *Chusan* sets sail at the end of this week," Wilson replied, "early Saturday morning. It will be a 90-day cruise, Mr. Barrington, bound for Hong Kong."

"Hong Kong?" Paul gasped. "You mean the one in China?"

Wilson chuckled drily. "Unless they've moved it, that's exactly what I mean."

"Then the answer is 'Yes,' Mr. Wilson. I'm your man!"

During the rest of that week, Paul had two important chores to attend to: he had to get his shot for yellow fever, and he had to give notice—such as it was—to his current employer, an Italian *artiste* known simply as Mr. Mario.

Although Mario owned this elegant salon, he was more or less content to live on his past reputation. He served as a kowtowing host to each newly arrived patron, but Paul never saw him touch a comb or a brush during his months of employment. As each new patron entered the salon, Mario would spring to the door, exclaim with delight in his effusive Latin manner, grab one of her hands, and standing on tiptoe, bow his head to plant a full-lipped kiss on the backs of her surprised fingers. Then, with a flourish, he would whisk off her coat and ask her to turn around while he stood with one hand on his hip and the other thoughtfully rubbing his chin. More often than not, the patron would seem terribly embarrassed by all this attention, as Mario stood there scrutinizing her for long, silent moments before finally springing to action. With a smile, he would usher the patron into the salon and call out, "Paul, this way please — front and center!" He would often lapse into such military commands though, to Paul's knowledge, there was no military in Mr. Mario's background.

At the close of business that Wednesday, Paul approached his employer with much trepidation. He had heard talk of Mario's infamous temper and, indeed, had witnessed a few of his "scenes" in person. First, he explained about the grand opportunity he was being given to work aboard a luxury liner. To his surprise, Mr. Mario seemed delighted for him.

"You are going to be a ship's hairdresser, Paul? Ah, how lucky you are! I, too, had that honor for several years, working on the most fabulous liner of them all, just before the war broke out. The *Normandie!* Now, that was luxury, my boy, and wall-to-wall glamour. Believe me, I dealt only with the wives and mistresses of billionaires and world-famous movie stars. For four long years, it was like a dream come true. Yes, I am very happy for you, dear boy. When will they be wanting you?"

"Well, that's what I wanted to talk to you about, Mr. Mario. It's to be quite soon."

"Oh? You mean, perhaps, the end of the month?" That current month still had three weeks to go.

"No, I'm sorry," Paul muttered. "It's more like the end of this week. First thing Saturday morning."

At that, Mr. Mario let out a long, wailing shriek that scared the devil out of everyone in the shop.

"*Santa Maria!*" he groaned. "You are giving me three days' notice?"

"I'm sorry, Mr. Mario, but that's when the ship sails. What else am I to do? Surely, you wouldn't want me to lose out on an opportunity like this, would you?"

Mario went silent for a moment, and it appeared as if he were mulling something over in his head. "I'll tell you what, Paul. There's one last favor you can do for me before you take off. If you agree to do as I ask, I'll agree to give you a good reference."

"You mean you won't if I don't?" asked Paul, thinking this sounded suspiciously like blackmail.

"Well, I'm not saying 'yes' or 'no' to that. But really, Paul, only three days' notice—not very professional, is it?"

Paul eyed him skeptically. "Okay, what's the favor?"

Mario gave him a beaming smile. "The royal family of England has need of your services as a barber."

Paul stared at him. "Could you throw that at me again, please?"

"Well, technically speaking, it's not the royal family, but it is one of the King's Coldstream Guards who has need of your attention. Except for you, I don't have anyone nearly experienced enough to take on this project."

"But that's not true, Mr. Mario. We're all barbers in this shop. That's part of our training."

"Yes, I know. But I've asked a few others, and since this duty is not compulsory, I must say their attitudes were most uncooperative."

"Well, that seems rather odd, doesn't it?"

"Not really. You see, the man you'll be shaving died of a heart attack about this time yesterday."

"Wait a minute," said Paul, who wasn't sure he had heard correctly. "Are you saying you want me to shave a corpse?"

"As a parting kindness to me, Paul, I certainly wish you would. It would add such a touch of prestige to the shop if one of my people did the honors. Naturally, the family wants him to look his best while he's lying in state."

"Oh, naturally . . ."

"He's all decked out in his uniform, you know, which is that wonderfully vivid cardinal red. But it seems he had a rather heavy beard, and perhaps you didn't know it, but most men's beards keep on growing a day or two after they've breathed their last."

"No, actually, I didn't know that," said Paul, fighting hard to swallow the nausea he'd felt at the very mention of this grisly idea. "In fact, I've never even seen a corpse before, much less gotten close enough to give it a shave. But off-hand, it seems to me this is a job for the embalmers. I mean, they've been fiddling around with the bloke anyway, so why can't they grab a razor and hop to it?"

"Out of the question," said Mario. "There are two different trade unions involved here. They figure they're not asking a barber to pump the cadaver full of formaldehyde, so why should *they* be expected to do anything tonsorial?"

"I'm sure that would make a lot of sense to me," said Paul, "if I didn't feel like throwing up at the moment."

"Nevertheless, that's the deal," said Mario, his tone going abruptly nasty. "You either shave that royal corpse, or you'll get no letter of reference from me."

Although Paul knew he could count on Professor Belmont's full support, he also realized his job with Mr. Mario was the very first professional assignment he'd ever had after serving his apprenticeship. Perhaps it was little enough to ask of him, since he was, in a manner of speaking, leaving the poor man in the lurch.

"Oh, what the hell," he said with a jaunty shrug. "I guess there's got to be a first time for everything. And who knows? Maybe an experience as gruesome as this one'll help to shape my character."

"That's the spirit, my boy!" Mr. Mario looked all sunny and smiling again. "You can go there right after dinner."

"Couldn't I make it before I eat?"

"Oh, of course. I suppose that would be best. They've got him at the St. Britannia Funeral Parlor on Oxford Street. He's all laid out and waiting for you."

"Waiting patiently, too, I'll wager."

"Now, let's not be naughty, dear boy," Mario wagged a finger at him. "Let's have some respect for the dead."

Easy for *you* to say, Paul thought as he went to the back and grabbed his kit. A half hour later, Paul entered his assigned "theater of operation." The person who greeted him looked funereal enough to be a mortician, which he was.

"Are you the man from Mr. Mario's shop?"

"Yes, sir. My name is Barrington."

"You seem a bit young for a job like this. Have you ever done this sort of thing before?"

"Well, I'm fully professional and I've given a lot of shaves in my time, and I suppose one or two of my patrons might have slept through it, but that's as close as I ever came to this kind of experience. Of course, those customers were able to get up and walk away after I finished with them."

"That's where all similarity ends," said the man, his voice a low and lugubrious drone. "Come with me, please. We've got him in our Coldstream Slumber Room."

Lovely, Paul thought as he followed the man down a long and sweet-smelling corridor of mirrors. There were elaborate displays of flowers everywhere, though Paul resisted the urge to ask who died.

13

When they reached the point of rendezvous, the doors were already open. There lay Paul's customer, the corpse with the five o'clock shadow. He was spread out flat on a table, all buttoned up in his beautifully tailored uniform.

"As you can see, we took him out of the coffin for you."

"Much obliged," said Paul. "It would have been a bit sticky if I'd had to crawl in with him, what with the open razor and everything." Paul gave him a sickly little smile, but the mortician was gazing at his work of art too intently to take any notice.

"Doesn't he look splendid?" the man asked.

"I'm sure he does," said Paul, "but not having seen the chap before, I don't have much to compare him with."

"Oh, believe me, he looked positively ghastly when they brought him here. He died of a coronary occlusion, you know, and it was several hours before they found the body. Actually, it was his pet dog who found him first, and it was such a shock for the poor animal he had a fit of nervous diarrhea and fainted dead away. You see, he had gone quite blue and scaly all over, and there was all this foam and spittle streaming out of his mouth. Of course, to look at him now you'd never believe it."

"The dog?"

"No, the deceased!"

Feeling a bit lightheaded, Paul said, "Could we please get on with it?"

"Certainly. But first I must give you some pointers."

"You mean, about shaving?"

"No, I mean about shaving *him,* your first dead customer. For one thing, you'll be shaving a totally different kind of skin."

"How different? I mean, aside from the fact that he's dead all over anyway."

"You will find that his skin is not malleable," he said.

"Oh? Meaning what, exactly?"

"If you flick it, it won't flick back."

Paul nodded. "Oh, I see. You mean it doesn't have the elasticity it had while he was living."

"Precisely. It has been set permanently in place by our team of mortuary cosmeticians. Therefore, you must proceed very carefully. One false move, and it would be tantamount to distorting a freshly sculpted bust modeled in clay."

"Well then, lucky for me it's his face I'll be shaving, and not his bust."

The mortician glared at him like a circling vulture. "Mr. Barrington, let's remember that this is a serious matter. This man died in service to the King!"

"Yes, sir, and God save him; but if there aren't any more 'pointers,' could I please do what I came for?"

"Certainly, after this one last warning: make sure you don't cut him."

"Oh? But surely he wouldn't bleed, would he? I mean, you certainly must have pumped all the blood out of him by now."

"It's not what we've pumped out of him I'm talking about; it's what we've pumped into him. One wrong slice, and he will squirt some of our most expensive embalming fluid all over you."

"Is that a fact? What color?"

"A sort of bile yellow."

Paul swallowed some of his own bile and took two giant steps into the room. "I promise, sir, I'll be very careful."

"Then I will leave you to your task," said the man, and turned to go.

"Wait a minute," Paul said, feeling a touch of panic. "You mean I'll be doing this all by myself?"

"Nonsense, Mr. Barrington. You don't really imagine you'll be alone in here, do you?" Not waiting for an answer, he gave Paul a gaseous parting smile and left the room, closing the door behind him.

Paul turned for a closer look at his subject. For courage, he decided to whistle, but his mouth was so dry he couldn't manage a proper pucker. So he sang snatches of some half-remembered popular tunes. He started with "I'll Never Smile Again" and ended up with "I'll Walk Alone." Reaching into his bag of tools, he withdrew shaving cream and razor. Up close, he realized this would be the first soldier he'd ever shaved who wore both lipstick and rouge. In their efforts to make the poor man look alive, they'd gone a bit wild with their paintbrushes.

Hating the ominous silence in the room, he decided to chat with his client as if he were still living. "How's it going, mate? Once over lightly will do it for you, right? Well, *do* try to hold still." Then Paul heard himself laughing as he added, "One false move and I'll cut you dead!" Lord, he thought as he heard the sound of his own giggles, I'm getting delirious.

Moving very carefully, he proceeded to lather the corpse up. The skin was so cold to his touch, it gave Paul a chill. And the face was so stiff and set, it was like working with a putty mask. As he worked, Paul felt more eerie and edgy by the moment. I'm really coming down with terminal goose pimples, he thought. Finally, there was only one precarious area left to shave, and that was around the man's neck. Paul remembered the warning not to soil his uniform, but it would be quite a trick to shave his neck without dripping lather on the high collar.

There was nothing for it but to crawl up on the table with the corpse. There was just enough room for him to kneel over its upper half and sustain exactly the leverage he needed to complete this delicate operation. A little astonished that he could refrain from trembling, Paul was just about finished when he accidentally lost his balance and let his elbow lean against the cadaver's midsection.

That's when it happened.

One prod in the belly and the corpse sat straight up, the mouth opening to emit a very gross and audible belch, a sound that went something like, *"BLULRRPP!"*

"Good Christ in Heaven!" Paul cried, lurching backward, falling off the table and pissing in his pants, all in the same split-second. Ignoring his own trail of urine, Paul flung open the door and ran screaming out of the hall. "Someone call a doctor, hurry! This man is still alive!"

It was quite a while before they were able to calm him down. Patiently, they explained what had happened. It had been an accumulation of air in the corpse's stomach that had caused him to sit up when Paul's elbow tapped him in the gut. "And as he did so, his mouth fell open and he passed air," added the mortician. "It's really a very natural phenomenon."

"Natural or unnatural, I'm not going back in there," said Paul. "He's all finished anyway. All he needs is a bit of mopping up."

The mortician gave him a superior smirk. "I must say, you're being rather thin-skinned, aren't you?"

"You're absolutely right," said Paul. "Thin-skinned, that's me. And as long as I have any say in the matter, that's just the way I plan to keep it."

Paul would always remember that gala send-off during the last days before he set sail on his first voyage as ship's hairdresser. That Friday night, his family and some of his old buddies from the RAF gave him a festive going-away party. The story of the corpse who sat up and burped was now perfect party conversation. And now that Paul was no longer frightened out of his wits, he even confessed to wetting his drawers for the first time since infancy. "It may be funny now," he said, laughing along with the rest, "but it certainly wasn't funny when it was happening. Remember, I was all alone in that room."

Early Saturday morning, he arrived at the dock and got his first look at the *Chusan*, a truly magnificent floating palace, painted creamy white. Although he didn't realize it at the time (since this was, after all, his first in-person glimpse of a luxury liner), the *Chusan* was a classic symbol of British luxury on the high seas that, with the advent of jet travel, would soon become a near-obsolete rarity. During the early Fifties, however, it was still in its heyday.

Never had Paul felt such a surge of excitement and anticipation as when he stepped on the gangplank and strode aboard. Just when he'd feared he would remain landlocked forever, he was actually doing it—leaving home and England to sail for foreign shores.

"Lord, I feel like I'm off to see the wizard!" he exclaimed aloud. Laughing behind him, a woman passenger said, "Then just follow the yellow brick road . . ."

Paul turned and smiled at her, and drank in the smiles of others boarding the ship along with him. All these friendly strangers, he thought, all sharing this grand adventure. It'll be like one big, happy floating family, ready to sink or swim together. Please, God, he prayed as he stepped aboard, don't spoil it all by getting me seasick!

THREE

For Paul Barrington, that first long voyage to the Orient and the South Pacific expanded into five long years of service aboard one sort of luxury liner or another. All in all, he traveled over 250,000 miles around the world, and in time he had the opportunity to style the hair and wigs of kings, queens, princes, movie stars, and even a few prime ministers. But, mostly, he remembered the fun he'd had when he wasn't getting into people's hair, during his many stopovers in port.

During those years, Paul found each new port a novel and heady experience. The rainbow-tinted coral of Fiji, the Maori natives of New Zealand, the marvelous shopping excursions in such cosmopolitan ports as Hong Kong, Singapore, Sydney, Melbourne, Rio, and Acapulco. Even during his second, third, and fourth voyages, he still found new things to intrigue him.

Paul discovered, too, that despite the many scenic glories to be found on any sea voyage, his most joyous times usually involved the people he met on board ship—the varied array of passengers and fellow seamen, as well as those he serviced in the shop. To be confronting all these strangers when they were on vacation meant that he was lucky enough to catch them at their very peaks of hope and enthusiasm. Most of the people Paul met on these voyages (although there were exceptions!) were always ready for new experiences. As a result, they were usually open-minded about forming friendly associations.

Like most clichés, the old adage that travel is broadening has a grain of solid truth in it. It's only natural that, with new sounds, sights, and environments to react to, all the responses to these experiences will be equally new. For Paul, most of those trips resulted in journeys of self-discovery, as well as providing him with a deeper comprehension of the world at large.

Despite Paul's excited and euphoric mood that first morning on the *Chusan*, he did have the presence of mind to report to Mr. Truesdale, the shop manager of the beauty salon, though he got lost twice before he found his destination.

Truesdale had a fat, round, amiable face and—at first glance—seemed to be a lot less temperamental and quirky than Mr. Mario, who, incidentally, *did* give Paul his much-deserved letter of reference. After Truesdale introduced Paul to his three co-workers, two guys who were close to Paul's age and a third who was a seasoned veteran in his late thirties, he took him around to meet the purser, the ship's doctor, and the chief steward. So far, Paul seemed to find these new associates quite congenial.

Mark Truesdale, a very chatty man in his mid-fifties, didn't hesitate to confide his most intimate secrets to Paul during their little tour. "I've *had* living on land, you know."

"Oh, really? Well, so have I."

"Yes, I've had two wives and two separate families, which grounded me until I was 45. Then I let them all fend for themselves and took my own brand of French leave, so to speak. Now, as far as I'm concerned, this is the only way to live—at sea and constantly in motion."

Much to Paul's surprise, Truesdale told him that on board ship, the hairdressing department and the gift shops were all combined, and that each concession was owned by the Ocean Trading Company. There were two such groupings on board, for first class and tourist passengers. Paul would be working in the first class section. But it came as a bit of a shock to learn that the salon staff was required to assist the gift shop manager both in selling and stocking the provisions needed for the voyage. The shops stocked everything from thumbtacks to fur coats, from chocolates to tennis rackets, and a great variety of luxury gift items like rare Dresden china, antique clocks, cameras, and jewelry.

"On a long voyage like this one, everything you could possibly think of has to be loaded on board," Truesdale told him. "You'd be surprised how many idiots aren't ready for the frequent change of climate we're bound to encounter. Which means they never have the proper clothes, and we have to be ready to sell them whatever they forgot to pack. Whatever merchandise we don't display in the shops or the salons has to be stored in the hold until there's further need. And because a new need crops up every day, part of your job will be to join the others every night after dinner in restocking the shelves in the shops."

Paul was a bit confused by this. "If I do all this work as a stock clerk, when do I find time to do any hairstyling?"

Truesdale threw back his head and laughed heartily at this. "Oh, Paul, you'll be surprised how much you can do when you know your whole career depends on it."

Paul chuckled a little, too, hoping desperately the man was kidding.

"But seriously, Paul, after a while, you'll welcome the variety these duties offer you. I mean, just think! When you're not catering to the hairstyling needs of the hundreds of passengers, plus the needs of a thousand-member crew, you'll have the chance to learn all you'll ever need to know about merchandising and doing inventory. It's a little like doubling in brass, I suppose, and in time you'll get to be a little double-jointed." Then he laughed again. "Or maybe it would help if you were just the tiniest bit schizophrenic, like the rest of us." Then he went serious again. "By the way, this is your first voyage, isn't it?"

"Yes, I'm afraid it is."

"No, I don't mean your first voyage as ship's hairdresser, I mean your first voyage, period."

With a sigh, Paul nodded. "That, too. Oh, I've been on the river in little cruises. The Thames, I mean."

"Yes," Truesdale muttered absently. "I didn't imagine you were talking about the Nile. Oh well, you'll probably throw up a lot the first few days, but please, if you feel you're about to heave, *do* try to make it to the head in time. Which won't be easy, as we have no private bathrooms in the shops. Although there's always the possibility of using one of the shampoo sinks as a *pissoir*, except there are usually too many people watching. Patrons, I mean. Now, where was I . . .?"

Smiling, Paul wondered if his slightly dotty old boss had been at sea a bit too long. "You needn't worry, sir. I've always had a cast-iron stomach." Even as he spoke, Paul tried not to recall the times he used to get hideously car-sick on buses as a little boy, especially the double-decker kind. But that had been eons ago.

After the manager had recited his long list of duties, Paul feared he'd be kept so frantically busy, he might get the feeling he was still slaving away on land. However, thanks to the steady, and not always tranquil, movement of the ship, this did not happen. Later, when he got his routine down solidly, he had more time to enjoy this extreme change of environment.

Paul also learned that he and his co-workers came under the jurisdiction of the captain, much like the ship's officers. This meant that Paul was given a comfortable tourist class cabin all to himself — or, rather, it *would* be comfortable, once he surmounted an initial misunderstanding about his bunk. It wasn't too spacious, mind you, but it was private.

He would also be allowed to dine in the main restaurant, like the ship's officers, along with the paying passengers. Since he wasn't in uniform as was the ship's crew, he figured his chances of meeting some lonely madcap of an heiress in need of company were pretty good. He could just hear himself whispering into her ear, "Why don't you come with me to my cabin so I can do your hair?" Not very romantic, perhaps, but it was definitely original.

During that first day, after Truesdale's long indoctrination tour and after Paul had enjoyed a brief, but lively, coffee break with his four co-workers, he was free to take a leisurely tour of his own. As he did, he tried hard not to reveal the boundless enthusiasm he was feeling, lest the passengers and crew suspect what a neophyte he was. But as he wandered about the magnificent vessel, he was literally enthralled every step of the way. The *Chusan's* first class section was the very last word in elegance. She had swimming pools, restaurants, ballrooms, bars, game rooms, super deluxe suites and every other possible luxury that could be squeezed into her 24,000-ton hull.

In later weeks, whenever he found time away from his duties, Paul never wearied of exploring every last nook and cranny of his massive new home. Despite the burden of his varied duties, what he enjoyed most of all was the stirring excitement he felt in just being a part of that vast sailing city. True, he worked damned hard all day long, and for long hours, but it still meant a great deal to him to know that he had a vital shipboard function to perform, as important in its way as the captain's and crew's duties.

Late at night, as he lay in his bunk, he would listen to the thrumming vibration of the engines down below, pacing the sound with the rhythm of his own pulsebeat, which made this new way of life more a part of him. During that first voyage, he experienced a feeling of expectation and suspense that he would recapture on each successive trip.

To be an integral part of the ship's personnel also gave him a feeling of urgent immediacy, as if everything he did during the day was of vital importance to every passenger and crew member on board. As a result, he felt a strong obligation to keep his methods of service as expert as he knew how.

When he realized there were a great many details about the running of a ship which he would have to learn on his own, Paul wasted little time in getting started. In his efforts to learn the language of sailing, he eventually memorized certain essentials. Starboard is the right side of the ship, facing the bow or forward end. Port is the left side of the ship. Weatherside or windward is the side of the vessel facing the wind, and lee or leeward is the side away from the wind. It was doubly important that he learn these things on his own, not only because nobody had time to teach him, but so that he could explain them to passengers, should they ask.

When the *Chusan* set sail that first morning, Paul stood on the boat deck, amidships port side, and watched the hundreds of strangers waving to the passengers from the dock while everyone tossed confetti back and forth. Paul had said goodbye to his family and friends at the send-off party the night before, urging them not to come to the dock, as he wanted no tearful farewells from his parents to mar the joy of this event. And how impossible it was for him to hide his excitement that morning! The tugboat that would push them into the Channel was already in position. Then the ship's horn blew a long blast, and throughout the vessel, the voice of a third mate could be heard yelling over the public address system, "All ashore that's going ashore! Quartermasters, to your stations!"

Suddenly, the silent giant came alive below and shuddered as her huge turbine engines began to turn. The spinning screws formed a whirlpool of foam at the stern of the ship. Mooring lines were released from ballards on the dock and hauled aboard. The ship was underway.

"Ship ahoy and so long, all you landlubbers!" Paul yelled over a second blast of the ship's horn. And to himself, he thought, I've made it—from now on, I'm a haircurling sailor, bound for the Orient, a latter-day Marco Polo, armed not with a sword, perhaps, but with a comb, brush and hair dryer that'll get me everywhere I want to go . . . for surely an adventure by any other name would still smell as sweet!

Paul had been warned to expect rough seas for the first few days, until they were well into the Mediterranean Sea. But he wasn't ready for his immediate reaction when the ship began to rock and roll, none too gently, from side to side. Within seconds, his mood changed from "Everything's Coming Up Roses" to "Everything's Coming *Up* . . . *!*" Determined not to let anyone see this sign of weakness, Paul kept his mouth tightly shut, despite his rising gut, and made a beeline for his cabin. He dashed into the room and leapt to the sink just in time to sacrifice his breakfast. Deciding to rest and get his breath, he flung himself on his bunk, then let out a yell. The mattress—if that's what it was—was as hard as cement. And the bunk seemed rather high, as he'd literally had to leap upward to get into it. Even more peculiar, there were no side rails to keep him safely tucked in. He wondered how he was expected to stay in bed during a storm. Sheer will power?

But he didn't want to start out his first day by launching a complaint, so he decided to tough it out until the next morning, a decision he would soon regret. After eight hours of precarious rolling and tossing, Paul felt that someone had made a terrible mistake in designing this cabin. He spent the whole night "navigating" in his bunk. Every time the ship rolled to one side, he almost went over the edge. He had nothing to hold onto except the sealed-shut porthole, which was very slippery to the grasp. As a result, instead of concentrating on being seasick, he spent all his energy trying to keep from falling asleep and thus running the risk of tumbling out of the bunk and onto his head. If that happened, he could well be facing his first day on the job with a touch of brain damage, and he did *so* want to make a good impression.

When Paul went to the dining room for some breakfast, he immediately recognized one of his new co-workers in the salon, a young Australian lad named Denny. He was 22, tall and angular, with kinky red hair, a pointed chin, and a real beak of a nose. To top that off, Denny also had a myopic squint and wore thick-lensed eyeglasses. This was only his second voyage as ship's hairdresser, so he wasn't exactly an old pro.

"'Morning, friend," said Denny, giving Paul a grin that was so unexpectedly ingratiating, it more than compensated for his other imperfections. "You look about as peaked as I feel. You been goin' the upchuck route, too, eh?"

"You mean, have I been seasick?" It was the first time Paul had even thought of this all night long.

"Please, don't use the word 'seasick,'" Denny begged him. "You wouldn't believe what a suggestible stomach I've got."

Paul smiled, thinking he was going to like this guy. He had a face right out of Dickens, and a sense of humor to boot.

"I was sick the first three days the last time, and then it just stopped," Denny told him, sipping some tea. "I'm hoping it won't last any longer this time around."

"Well, I did have a touch of vertigo," Paul admitted. "But then I had more urgent problems . . ."

"Urgent problems, my ass!" somebody said behind him. "That's no way to start a voyage." It was his boss, Mr. Truesdale, plus one of the other operators, Ned Allison. Ned was a portly, bookish little man in his late thirties who, like Truesdale, had been through the divorce wars and was now content to roam the seas.

Suddenly, it was a very cozy little breakfast party, and everything seemed so friendly, Paul hated to mention the fact that he hadn't slept a wink all night. Finally, he told them about the incredibly hard mattress and the bunk without rails.

"What's your cabin?" Truesdale asked him. "I mean, what's the number?" As soon as Paul told him, Truesdale let out a gasp. "My God, when I told the chief officer you'd be replacing Glenn Marshall, he really took me literally."

"Glenn Marshall," Paul said. "You mean, he was the man who was taken ill at the last moment?"

"Taken ill?" Truesdale asked, and suddenly he and the others were laughing fitfully. "Suddenly taken drunk would be more like it. You see, I had given him one last chance to get sober and stay that way, but he blew it. Glenn's problem was his inability to resist temptation whenever he went ashore."

"But what does that have to do with the condition of my bunk?" asked Paul.

"Well, he had other problems," said Truesdale.

"A bad back," Denny said.

"I think you should see the chief officer and have it taken care of," said Truesdale.

"No, Mark," said Ned Allison, "by rights, that's one of the duties of the night steward. You tell him to take the board out of that mattress, Paul."

"A board? You mean, that's what I was sleeping on? I mean, not sleeping on?"

"That, plus two mattresses," said Denny. "Except that board was on top of the second mattress. That's the way Glenn wanted it."

"Look, Paul," said Truesdale, "let's wait until we have our breakfast. Then you and I can go see the steward together. He can be quite difficult at times, and I know for a fact that Glenn Marshall gave him a lot of problems."

Half an hour later, Paul, Truesdale, and the night steward, a sour-faced man by the name of Whitney, were having more than a few words. When they registered their complaint about Marshall's former cabin, Mr. Whitney flew off the handle.

"What the hell *is* this? Every time they hire a new flit for the beauty parlor, I have to rebuild and redesign the goddamned bunk!"

Paul winced at the word "flit," though Truesdale had already warned him that Whitney, like a few others on board too ignorant to know any better, was one of those who assumed any male hairdresser had to be gay. "Sure, I could send him to my ex-wives to prove otherwise," Truesdale had mused later, "but why bother trying to impress that idiot?"

"Okay, Mr. Whitney," Truesdale said, "don't blow a gasket."

"That Marshall freak, he was the worst of the lot," Whitney was saying. "Two voyages ago, I had to have one of his mattresses thrown overboard. You want to know why?"

"Not especially," said Truesdale.

"Because it was full of piss stains!"

With that, Truesdale (who, Paul was learning, could be an outrageous tease) deliberately stamped his foot like a caricature of some burlesque drag queen and said, "Pulleeze, Mr. Whitney, language like that offends my sensibilities!"

Paul had to turn away to keep from laughing.

" . . . I'm tellin' you," Whitney went on, "that old fruit was so drunk most of the time, he used to piss the whole night away in his sleep. He coulda' drowned himself, for Christ's sake. Then, during this last trip, the bastard suddenly complained about back troubles and insisted we put a board over the springs of two of the hardest mattresses I could find . . ."

"Look, Whitney," Truesdale interjected, his attitude going very stern, "we don't care about the problems you had with anyone else. It so happens that Mr. Barrington here is a new employee on board this ship, and he would appreciate it if you would replace those two hard mattresses with one soft one, take that board and chop it up for kindling, and then install proper side rails on the bunk to keep him from falling on his ass and suing the hell out of the P&O Shipping Line, and dragging *you* into court as the cause of it all. Now, if that's not clear to you, Mr. Whitney, I'll go right to the chief officer and repeat it, word for word."

After a long, tense moment of silence, Whitney finally muttered, "No, that won't be necessary. I'll make the changes myself."

"When?" Truesdale demanded.

"Within the hour, okay?"

With that, Truesdale beamed at him and went into his "pansy" mimicry act again, one hand on hip, the other a limp wrist, waving in the air. "Thanks oodles, doll . . . see 'ya later!"

With that, he simpered off, Paul hurrying after him. Not until they were out of sight did Paul let go with gales of laughter. "What a performance! But tell me, aren't you just adding grist to the mill by doing all that swishy stuff in front of him?"

"Who cares?" Truesdale said in his normal voice. "As long as *we* know what we are, is it so important that toads like Mr. Whitney should bother us?" Then, as an after-thought, he eyed Paul a bit shrewdly. "I say, *you're not,* are you? I mean, if you are, it's nobody's business. And, like I always say, to each his own, as long as you don't do it in

front of the customers and frighten the horses . . . ," laughing madly again, " . . . and believe me, some of them are
very horsey!"

"No," Paul said, "I'm not, to answer your question. In
fact, until now, it never occurred to me that anyone would
have reason to ask me, just because of the work I do."

"Lord, this *is* your first voyage, isn't it?" Truesdale
remarked, not unkindly. "Well, you're in international
waters now, Paul, so you had best prepare yourself for a
whole world full of nasty little bigots like our Mr. Whitney.
The point is not to let yourself stoop to their level by trying
to prove how wrong they are. You have to tell yourself that
the opinions such people have of you don't matter one bit."

Paul smiled at this philosophy. "You mean, I shouldn't
go around fighting to prove my manhood."

"Of course not. And besides, there's really only one way
you'd want to do that, in bed with the lady of your choice."

"Ah, now you're playing my song," Paul laughed. On
impulse, he added, "You know something, Mr. Truesdale?
If I've got to have a boss, I'm bloody glad as hell it's you,
because I'm beginning to suspect you're a very nice man."

"Watch it, buster," scowled Truesdale, "that sounds pretty
queer to me." That set them to laughing again. "But, for
God's sake, stop this 'Mr. Truesdale' stuff. From now on,
I'm just Mark, okay?"

"Okay, Mark," said Paul. "It's a deal."

That night, Paul's bunk was equipped with side rails, one
soft new mattress, and no board. Now that the first big
hurdle of his maiden voyage had been overcome, he felt
confident that the remainder of the cruise would be on
glass-smooth waters.

But, as he would discover during this, his first experience
as an innocent abroad, fate really threw the book at him.

FOUR

At the time it was happening, Paul figured that after his first cruise at sea, all his succeeding voyages would have to seem easier. The best thing that happened involved the good friends he made among the staff. Although he got on well with his co-workers, he saw so much of them during the day that he made friends after hours with people who worked in various other parts of the ship. As a result, it was the purser, Jason Rutledge, and his assistant, a man by the name of John Derringer, who became Paul's closest comrades during his forays ashore.

He remained good buddies, meanwhile, with the other guys working in the shop, particularly the irrepressible Denny and his boss, Mark Truesdale. The other man in his early twenties whose name was Roy Tolliver, was the only other Londoner, aside from Paul, working in the shop. He appeared to be more quiet and aloof than the others, and kept much to himself during his free time. Eventually, Paul learned that Roy had resented his being hired from the first, feeling that such a newcomer didn't deserve to be given a spot in the first class salon right off the bat—suggesting it was only a freak bit of luck that put Paul where he was. When Paul realized that was the reason for Roy's antipathy, he decided it was just too silly to think about.

"Don't think too badly of him, Paul," said Mark Truesdale, who was quick to come to anyone's defense. "He's a very bitter young man. The story goes that he and his wife had owned a very chic salon together in London, but she up and ran away with one of their best customers. When

31

he got home one night, she had cleaned out all her belongings. It seems she left him only a brief note that said, "Sorry, Roy, but Jackie and I are madly in love and there's nothing you can do to change that." The poor beggar, no wonder he felt so suicidal. When he was offered this assignment, he sold everything and shipped out. And now it seems he doesn't trust a soul."

"You say she ran off with one of their best customers? Then surely Roy must have known the man."

"Oh, no, Paul, if this had been a man, I'm sure Roy would have been able to deal with it a lot better."

Paul stared at him. "Good Lord, you don't mean . . . ?"

Mark nodded.

"Poor devil," said Paul. "My God, what a low blow it must be, to have the woman you love choose another woman over you. How on earth do you fight it?"

"Well, you don't. If you're like Roy, you just get very bitter. So do let's be kind to the poor battered man the next time he's being especially nasty."

"I'll try, Mark. I promise."

As for his buddy, Jason Rutledge, the ship's purser, Paul found no such barriers of malice or hypersensitivity. Jason was a tall, wiry, dashing sort of fellow, with curly blond hair, rakish good looks, a charming blue-eyed smile, and a thoroughly winning manner. Jason's only weakness was women, for he was powerfully sexed and rarely let an opportunity go by to put his hungers to the test. Nonetheless, Paul found him to be one of the most entertaining guys he'd ever met. While it was true he had a devilish sense of humor, he was never intentionally cruel or malicious. And he knew his job, right down to the last detail. Despite the difference in their ages—Jason was 33—he and Paul hit it off right from the start, confiding in one another, sharing meals or drinks at the bar, and making some memorable trips ashore when they were in port.

Paul's first cruise had been launched at the peak of the summer vacation season, in early June, which explained why the *Chusan* was even more crowded and frantic than usual. At that time of year, it seemed to Paul that just about everybody and his mother-in-law wanted to sail off for ports unknown. And who was doing most of the traveling? Women, naturally, bless them! In this case, there was an extra contingent of American ladies in one enormous tour group who had just completed an extensive Grand Tour of Europe and were now ready to invade the Orient and the South Pacific.

Many of these ladies were in their fifties and sixties, the hearty souls who had outlived their husbands by at least a decade. Paul had to learn very quickly how to deal with these hordes of matrons, spinsters, and randy little widows, many of whom looked so eager to "get away from it all," you'd think they were on the lam. As Mark explained it to him, it was like an annual stampede — females on the hoof, all of them demanding "personal attention" from the ship's hairdressers, especially those who were as young and tempting as Paul Barrington. He had a habit of smiling pleasantly at all his customers, but how could he know the way in which so many of these flesh-hungry matrons interpreted that little courtesy?

Some of them were so bold and aggressive, Paul didn't always know how to handle them. On that trip, there was one glittering lady in her mid-forties who, when she introduced herself, readily admitted that her dear, dead husband had left her most of the oil wells in Texas (which, Paul thought, explained her curious accent). This woman was very blond, busty, and sensual-looking, and she removed such a collection of diamonds and emeralds before he did her hair, it made him very nervous just watching them sparkle as he worked.

"I always feel so naked whenever I strip off my jewels," she told him. "Do you think that's silly?"

"No, indeed, Madam," he said gallantly. "You may strip off anything you like. Within reason, that is."

She howled wildly at that, whereupon Paul draped the curtain around her stall and proceeded to get her hair ready for a wash.

It was then that the Texas baroness made her move. "Now look, Buster," she said, her voice going low and mock-threatening, "I'm very fussy about my hair . . ." To his horror, she reached down between his legs and grabbed him solidly by the balls, holding them firmly in her grasp for a moment. ". . . So you'd better do an extra good job on me, 'cause I'm dining with the captain tonight and, when he looks at me, I want him to know what a princess he's got on his hands, you follow my line 'a thinking? If you screw up my looks, I'll know just where to hurt you." Then she gave his astonished credentials one last squeeze and set them free.

She eyed his face in the mirror and let out some more of her Texas guffaws. "What's the matter, honey? You look a little nonplussed. Didn't bruise your li'l ol' pomegranates, did I?"

"Not a bit, Madam," he said hoarsely. "Of course, I was just about to turn soprano before you let them go, but now, as it happens, there's no harm done." That got her laughing so raucously, Paul felt sure the others in the shop were wondering what was tickling this lady.

He finally got her calmed down enough to do her hair, although he continued to tingle in the groin all through the operation. Perhaps if he'd been more experienced, he might have chucked her out on her ass as soon as she grabbed him. And then, when he realized it didn't actually hurt, he was rather intrigued by the idea. No woman had ever reached through to him in quite that manner before, not even in his steamiest fantasies. But if it happened again, he hoped he would first be given a little warning. He wondered if he shouldn't equip himself with one of those metal jockstrap "cups" like the football players wore. One never knew how vulnerable one could be, standing next to a customer, ripe for plucking (so to speak). Before she left the salon, and after tipping him extra generously, the Texas grabber said, "I'd like to see you again in more intimate circumstances, hon'. You think that could be arranged?"

"Of course, Madam," he winked back, "but only if you promise to cut your fingernails." That sent her roaring and howling out of the shop.

When she was gone, Denny raced over to him. "Good Lord, Paul, what's the story there? What the hell did you do to keep that old cow laughing so hard?"

"She just found me terribly amusing," Paul said blithely. Then he winced as he felt a residual throb from below.

As it turned out, that experience was a "one-shot deal." In the future, most of the ladies he encountered in the line of duty found much subtler ways to reveal their interest in him. In time, Paul tried to abstain from getting too playful with anyone with whom he was professionally involved, preferring to release those inhibitions only while he was in port, among total strangers. But that was not always a rule he found easy to abide by.

On the first night of most voyages, there was usually some sort of dinner, dance, or cocktail party planned by the ship's social director. At these *soirées*, everyone seemed so fiercely determined to get acquainted that the jabbering bedlam of voices and human traffic set Paul's teeth on edge.

While it was true that many of the women seemed to belong to that sorority of geriatric swingers called senior citizens, Paul often found a much greater age range than he anticipated. Seated at his table during that first voyage was a delightfully overdeveloped teenaged girl. She was militantly chaperoned by her mother, of course, a buxom and officious-looking divorcée of fifty-plus who'd been having lusty thoughts about Paul ever since he gave her a facial and a henna rinse earlier that day. During the rest of the voyage, it seemed, wherever he looked, there she was, giving him adoring looks and panting. The fact that he was always very crisp and professional with her didn't seem to deter her. She was out for the kill.

These two, by the way, had come to the *Chusan* direct from a lifetime engagement in a place called Kalamazoo, Michigan: Bertha Burlington and her daughter, Suzy — the latter suffering from one of the most advanced cases of erotic precocity Paul had ever observed. The kind of kid who was 16 going on 40. That child chased everything male on the ship, including stewards, waiters, officers, and even one of the assistant pursers who was fool enough to let her catch him one dark and windy night up on the poop deck.

It was Jason Rutledge, the Purser, who told Paul about this incident. "John Derringer, that idiot! He actually came to me to help him fight her off. I told him he could go to prison for child molesting if her mother ever found out. But he said there was no real molesting involved — seems the kid knew how to have her way with him without endangering her maidenhead. Afterwards, he said he gave her a good dressing down. Warned her not to kiss Mommy goodnight until she'd had a good gargle."

"Now, that's incredible," said Paul.

"Is it really? Why?"

"Because that girl's mother's been telling me how she plans to enter the girl in a convent as soon as they get back home."

"Well, that explains why the kid's in such a hurry to get all her licks in before Mamma lowers the boom."

One night, Paul also met a particularly adventurous female at his table, by the name of Katie Fountainhead. He later learned she was actually the elected water commissioner of a good-sized town in Indiana. She was a rare bird, indeed, a veritable water fowl, as it turned out. A bit later that night, Paul and Jason Rutledge were having a drink together in the ship's main cocktail lounge when Bertha Burlington hurried over to them. She was a bit breathless and excited about something.

"Oh, there you are, Mr. Rutledge," she said. "I've been looking all over for you. I didn't want to report this to one of your assistants." Suddenly she spotted Paul. "And you, too, Mr. Barrington. How nice!"

"You wanted to see me on business, Mrs. Burlington?" asked Jason, clearly not in the mood to be hearing any more passengers' complaints that day.

"Well, it's not all that confidential," she said. "I mean, since Mr. Barrington is here, too, I'd feel better if I confided in both of you. You both have that same kind of warmth and understanding in your eyes." The way she was ogling Paul, it was clear she felt a lot more heat generating from him than she did from the purser.

"Let's go over in the corner and share a table," Paul said. At once, he saw the disappointed frown on the face of the chief bartender, Clyde Allenby. Clyde loved a good gossip, and it looked as if this bit of dirt was being swept out of earshot.

When they were settled at a booth, the young Italian waiter, Alonzo, came over and Mrs. Burlington ordered a Pink Lady, while Paul and Jason had two more Scotch and sodas. The fact that Paul wouldn't turn 21 for another six weeks didn't seem to limit his supply of evening highballs, certainly not when he was so frequently accompanied by the ship's purser.

"Now, tell us, dear," said Jason, "what's bothering you? Not your daughter, I hope."

"Oh, goodness, no! Suzy's the last of my worries."

On hearing this, Paul wondered if mothers were always the last to know. Judging by the gossip he'd heard about little Suzy, she was fast becoming the champion bed-hopper on the ship.

"No, it's Miss Fountainhead," said Mrs. Burlington. "I've something awful to tell you about her."

"That sweet little lady?" Paul asked. "That's hard to believe."

"Sweet? Oh, Mr. Barrington, you don't mean to tell me she's your type? Not that scrawny old thing . . ."

"Paul didn't say she was his type, Mrs. Burlington," Jason quickly came to his rescue. "He just said she was sweet."

"Right," said Paul. "There must be a great many other sweet women on board this ship who aren't my type."

"Okay," said Jason, "so what's your problem?"

"It is *her* problem, Mr. Rutledge. It's certainly not mine." She glanced furtively to the right and left before going on. "Oh, gentlemen, it's such an indelicate matter, I don't know if I can bring myself to talk about it."

"Force yourself," said Jason, giving Paul a fast wink.

"Very well. It seems that Miss Fountainhead has a 'thing' about johns."

The two men exchanged a quick and wary glance. "Come again?" said Jason.

Mrs. Burlington sat up straighter, thrusting her pontoon-sized bosom outward with the air of a lady in the midst of a painfully proud civic duty. "She inspects them, the silly fool. Whenever I happen to see her on the ship, there she is, doing it again. It's like some sort of addiction with her. I mean, she does this in public, gentlemen. Don't you think it's a scandal?"

"Wait a minute," said Paul, "I think I'm a little confused here."

"What you're saying," said Jason, "is that Miss Fountainhead inspects rest rooms, right?"

"Exactly!" she said. "Frankly, I've been hoping someone in authority would do something about it by now, but it seems that nobody else cares. Anyway, I've been on the same tour with this woman for months now, and whenever she boards a ship, or a plane or a train, for that matter, she has this unsavory compulsion to inspect each and every comfort station. More than once, I've caught her in the act—you know, flushing toilets and trying out soap dispensers, or testing the hand dryers or the comparative wet strength of the tissues and paper towels . . ."

"Good heavens," hissed Paul in mock alarm, "how sick can you get?"

"Yes, that was *my* reaction, too. It's getting very irritating. Of course, my daughter thinks it's funny, but I don't think it's so funny. Do you, gentlemen? Actually, it's quite sad. I feel sorry for anyone that disgusting and, well, as you said, Mr. Barrington, just plain sick. You *will* speak to her about it, Mr. Rutledge, won't you?"

Jason gave her a patient smile. "I don't think it's anything to get so overwrought about. After all, this lady isn't hurting anyone, is she?"

"Not yet. But how can we predict what will happen, once this thing comes to a head?"

Paul couldn't believe she actually said that last line with a straight face.

"Ever since we began this voyage, she's been hopping from deck to deck, cabin to cabin, just so she can audition the plumbing. It's all so morbid, I feel like swooning every time I follow her and catch her doing it. You don't suppose it could have anything to do with her early toilet training, do you?"

Still retaining his patient smile, Jason said, "Tell me, as far as you know, has Miss Fountainhead stayed out of the men's rooms?"

Mrs. Burlington gasped, and so did Paul, to keep from giggling. "Well, I should certainly hope so! But, my goodness, you don't really suppose . . . ?"

"No, I do not," Jason said. "Which means she's not really breaking any laws. She's simply a very fastidious person. Is that a crime?"

"Or, perhaps, back in her home town, that's part of her job," said Paul. "Remember, she's a water commissioner."

"Right," said Jason. "Which means she could have been assigned to do a sort of survey, lavatories around the world, or something of that nature. Anyway, I promise you, Mrs. Burlington, the very first time I catch Miss Fountainhead flushing the urinals in the men's john, I'll really give her what-for, okay?"

"Well, I never . . . !" said the woman indignantly. "Talk about favoritism, Mr. Rutledge! Tell me, what's that skinny old virgin got that I haven't?"

"My dear Mrs. Burlington," Jason said coolly, "if, as you say, Miss Fountainhead is a virgin, I believe you've just answered your own question."

With that, she shot to her feet and glared furiously at both of them. But she was apparently at a slight loss for words. All she could manage was another "Well, I *never!*" and she stormed hastily out of the bar.

When she was gone, Paul and Jason let out such roars of laughter that Clyde Allenby insisted they come back to the bar and let him in on the fun. When he'd heard the story, he said, "Hey, I wouldn't be surprised if she went straight to the captain and told him his chief purser is making waves with a lady plumber."

"Let her, the silly bitch," said Jason. "Instead of putting a leash on that nymphet daughter of hers, she wastes my time and her own complaining about a perfectly harmless little lady who isn't bothering anybody."

Oddly enough, when Paul took the elevator to his own deck later that evening, he saw Miss Katie Fountainhead scampering down the corridor, making a beeline for the nearest ladies' room. Well, what of it, he thought. So the little lady had a hangup. He figured it was *her* vacation, so she was entitled. And no matter how odd this habit was, at least it had been "consenting partners," just Katie and the pipes.

On the other hand, if she ever stopped testing the appliances and started turning on other ladies, well, maybe then both Jason and the captain would have something to worry about. But until then, he felt Miss Katie Fountainhead should be allowed to sail her own course.

They were three weeks out at sea during that first voyage when it occurred to Paul that he hadn't yet felt bored by what some people had warned him was the monotony of sea travel. When he wasn't fulfilling his varied and arduous duties, he found there was always a great diversity of shipboard activities he could enjoy. Just being able to meet new people every day continued to be an adventure for him. This was particularly the case when he joined the Early Risers Coffee Club, which convened on the promenade deck every morning at 6:30. He remained a staunch member of this group during the voyage, as did Denny and Mark Truesdale. It was often at that ungodly hour of the morning that Paul managed to meet a fascinating melange of world travelers, each of them with a new story to tell. Another favorite pastime, mostly late at night, was to lean against the rail as he stood on deck and looked out over the ocean, convinced anew that the sea was in his blood to stay and that he would never want to work on land again.

As for more adventures to be encountered on the job, they continued to surface in one guise or another, always when Paul least expected them. One morning, when some six members of the same tour group were in the salon having "the works," including facials, permanents, mud packs, and dye jobs, the ship was rocked by something very close to a disastrous tidal wave.

It had been smooth sailing for days when, from out of nowhere, a huge wave struck the starboard plates of the ship, causing it to list a good 30 degrees to port. At the moment of impact, Paul had just finished applying a neck-to-hairline mud pack to the face of Mrs. Bertha Burlington. The next thing he knew, he flew full-tilt into the lady's lap, accidentally smearing the last dab of mud right across her mouth. Bertha couldn't open her mouth to express her surprise and horror.

In that moment there was such up-ended bedlam in the salon that the whole place looked like ladies' night in a Turkish bath after a killer earthquake. The shock did something mischievous to the ship's plumbing, and all those dainty heads lowered for a shampoo were nearly drowned in spritzing geysers, sprouting toward the ceiling. My God, thought Paul, where is Katie Fountainhead when we really need her? In a flurry of flapping white bibs and towels, everybody began to scramble at once. But since the ship was listing so heavily, they had to fight gravity, among other obstacles in their way. Those who had been caught in the middle of a platinum blue rinse looked especially bizarre — detergent blue color on one side, and telltale gray on the other. It was as if three demon hags from *Macbeth* had suddenly cloned themselves all over the salon.

"Don't worry, ladies!" roared Mark Truesdale above the din. "I'll buy each of you a brand new wig as soon as we dock. In the meantime, everybody up to the main deck to be issued life preservers!"

"Is the ship sinking?" a lady yelled. "If it's not, I'm not going *anywhere* looking like this!"

"Of course we're not sinking," said Mark. "We're just listing a little. But for safety's sake, let's all file out of the shop in an orderly fashion." Since so few of the ladies could even stand up, Paul felt this was a purely rhetorical suggestion on Mark's part. But with the mere mention of the possibility that the ship might be sinking, sheer lunacy became the accepted order of the moment. Never had Paul heard such gasping and caterwauling, as towels flew off heads. Bodies of every dimension shot out of booths and out from under dryers, and went sliding backward along the floor. Despite the terror in the room, Paul heard cries more of vanity than of fear.

"I refuse to meet my maker looking like this," one lady yelled. "All my pores are open!"

"You expect me to be seen in public with half a henna rinse on my head? My God, I look like I've been put out to *rust!*"

Poor Mrs. Burlington was easily the unluckiest of the pack, since she was the only member of the group who couldn't put up a squawk. Her daughter, Suzy, in pink hair rollers, looked a bit more civilized, so she dutifully started dragging her mother toward the exit. With a bald-pate plastic cap on her head and black clay mottling her face, Bertha resembled a daring new addition to Mount Rushmore: Louis Armstrong in drag. She flopped around in her daughter's arms like a harpooned whale, issuing wild grunting noises from her throat and clawing frantically at the mud on her face, but her jowls remained so solidly encased, Paul felt sure it would take a sledge hammer to set her free.

It seemed amazing that all this commotion had only lasted a brief two minutes before they felt the sensation of the ship starting to balance itself out. People who had been sliding against walls could now stand up. "Glory be!" cried a picturesque Irish octogenarian. "It's all over! Come on, let's wash up and get out of here!"

But it was impossible to wash up. There was no water, and the electric power in the shop, too, was temporarily defunct.

"Look, Paul," said Mark, "God knows we can't make it up to the main deck. And now that everything's steady again, I don't see the need. Let's try to get them into the card room."

This was only a few doors down from the salon, so Paul, Mark, and the other operators proceeded to lead their capsized charges to the card room. But when they reached what they had hoped would be their safe harbor, the place looked as if a typhoon had hit it. The ship's doctor, a frazzled-looking man by the name of Dr. Albertson, was there with his nurse, Miss Joiner. With a glance Paul saw how desperately they were needed. There were men and women scattered in all directions, as well as overturned tables and chairs, handbags, a lost lady's shoe or two, even an ownerless pair of dentures. Fortunately, the majority of the injuries were minor despite the shambles. Those who had fainted were given quite a fright when they regained consciousness and saw the female freak show that had spilled in from the beauty salon. After a strong dose of smelling salts, one revived passenger glanced at Bertha Burlington in black face and then promptly lost consciousness again.

It was one full, frenzied nightmare of an hour before the water and power were restored and the ladies could flee back to the sanctuary of the salon to mop themselves up. By the time Paul dragged himself to his cabin that night, he was so exhausted, he collapsed into his bunk with all his clothes on.

At work the next morning, Paul figured he must have been feeling some residual hysteria from the events of the day before, as he still felt very jumpy and keyed-up. His first customer was a rather portly but aristocratic lady in her late fifties. She had such a regal bearing and such consummate poise, Paul was simply not prepared for her nose. It was easily the largest, longest and ugliest proboscis he had ever seen on a female, and the fact that this elegant *grande dame* seemed totally unaware that it was on her face completely did him in. Indeed, she strode through the salon as if she thought she was the most distinguished looking dowager on board.

Paul had only begun the preliminaries when he felt the giggles rising up in his throat. "I can't do it," he thought, going into a panic. "My God, what's happening to me? I can't look at this lady's nose and do her hair! Doesn't she realize that the only flattering coiffure I could create for her would have to be draped cleverly forward, over her face?"

With that thought, he managed to dismiss himself. "Back in a jiffy," he said, then sped out of her sight. He called Mark aside, and led him to a far corner of the shop.

"Mark, I'm sorry, I'm afraid you'll have to fill in for me over there."

Mark glanced at his customer and saw at once that she already looked both puzzled and annoyed. "What's up, Paul? Are you ill?"

"No, it's just that Mrs. Nosegay over there is too much for me this morning." He felt the delirium rising up again and turned away so he couldn't see her, even from afar. "I've never in my life seen a nose quite like that, Mark. And the bloody funny thing of it is, she doesn't seem to know it's there!"

"Oh, Paul, don't be so foolish," Mark said sternly. "Where's your sense of decorum? Remember, we are all professionals in this shop. The poor woman looks quite rattled already. Well, I'll calm her down in no time. After all these years, I fancy I've developed a rather tranquilizing bedside manner. I'll bring her a nice cup of tea and make her feel at home."

Paul watched from the corner, wanting to study this master diplomat in action. Mark hurried across the room and gave the lady one of his brightest smiles.

"Good morning, Mrs. Masters. How are we today?"

"I thought I was just fine, until your young hairstylist suddenly disappeared."

"Don't you worry about that," said Mark. "We'll bring you a little refreshment to make you feel more comfy."

She gave him a gracious smile. "Well, that does sound promising."

"Now tell me, Mrs. Masters, do you take cream or sugar in your nose?"

FIVE

During that first long cruise on the *Chusan*, Paul managed to memorize the extensive itinerary, wanting to do some advance reading in the ship's library so that he would know a little something about each port before he went ashore for a visit. On the first lap of their journey to Hong Kong, they would be stopping at Port Said, Aden — a port just the other side of the Suez Canal — and at Ceylon, Penang, Singapore, and Hong Kong. After a four-day stopover in Hong Kong, the ship would sail through the South Pacific and Polynesia, ending the tour in San Francisco. From Hong Kong, there would be stopovers in Japan, Taiwan, the Philippines, Samoa, Bora Bora, Tahiti, and Hawaii, and Paul was already booked to start the next tour with the P&O Line, which would take him to the Mediterranean.

Meanwhile, just a few days before they were due to dock in the port of Colombo, Ceylon, Paul found a way to break the ice with Roy Tolliver, his only co-worker who had remained persistently cold and unfriendly. Thinking that any man whose wife had run off with another woman was more to be pitied than censured, Paul had seized every opportunity to make friends with the man. But Roy had continued to be very abrupt and cool in his presence.

Then, one morning at the shop, when Paul had just finished with a customer and had some free time until his next appointment, he happened to notice Roy, who was busily giving a woman a permanent. Like most of the ladies who could afford these expensive cruises, this one was wonderfully chic and sophisticated looking, with that "high gloss" look that came only with the territory of the rich and the privileged. Admiring the assured technique Roy applied in his work, Paul casually watched for a moment. Roy had already fastened the curlers in her hair and applied the special permanent wave solution.

As Paul watched, he noticed a curler on the floor next to the customer. That in itself wasn't too odd, except that the longer he looked at the curler, the more certain he was that it had a bit of hair clamped within it. A moment later, he saw another curler drop to the floor. This time there was no mistaking where it had dropped from: the head of Roy's glamorous customer.

On the pretext of going to the drinking fountain, Paul nonchalantly walked by and bent to pick up the curler. As he did, another one dropped to the floor nearby. Each curler had a generous slice of hair inside of it. Paul knew he would have to act fast if he wanted to help Roy avert a tragedy.

Keeping his tone light and casual, he went to Roy and said, "I say, old friend, there's a couple of your curlers on the floor."

Roy gave Paul a hostile glance, as if to say, Must you be so pushy? Aloud, he said, "Don't worry about it. I'll pick them up in a minute."

He has no idea what I'm trying to tell him, thought Paul. He couldn't very well yell out, "If you don't stop what you're doing, the permanent you're giving this lady will leave her permanently *bald!*" How could he warn Roy without alarming the customer?

When he gave it more thought, Paul was able to figure this situation out, knowing it was something that could happen to any hairstylist and, indeed, had almost happened to him on more than one occasion. This lady had obviously been dyeing her hair. But when Roy asked her about it, which all hairdressers are trained to do before deciding which permanent wave solution to use, the customer must have fibbed to him, perhaps out of vanity. If she had told him the truth, Roy would have used a specially diluted solution meant expressly for dyed hair. But she hadn't, and because he had believed her, Roy had used the regular solution which was clearly much too strong, considering the condition of her hair.

"And now look at her," thought Paul as he watched Roy continue the damage. "It's enough to curl all the hair right off of her head."

One thing was certain, he would have to get Roy's attention fast while there were still a few strands left on that woman's head to curl. If Roy continued, his customer could well walk out of the salon looking like a female Daddy Warbucks!

"Oh, Mr. Tolliver," Paul called out, "could you come over here, please? There's a phone call for you in the office."

Roy gave him a frosty stare, then quickly excused himself and hurried across the room. Paul beckoned him into one of the booths.

"What's going on here, Barrington? You know as well as I do that we're not allowed any personal phone calls while on duty."

Paul took out one of the curlers with hair, which he'd kept in his pocket. "Look at this, Roy. What does it tell you?"

Roy examined the curler in his hand. Then he glanced through the entrance of the booth and observed the many other curlers on the floor, next to his customer. "Oh, my God," he said, "her hair is falling out!" He went pale and his body slumped, until Paul was certain he was about to faint. He grabbed him under the arms, just in time.

"Are you all right, Roy?" The poor guy looked near collapse. He tried to speak several times before he could get a word out.

"What will I do?" he cried. "If I go over there and tell her what's happening to her hair, she's liable to jump overboard. In fact, right this minute, that's what *I* feel like doing."

"Now, get a grip on yourself, Roy," Paul said. "Take a few deep breaths. Then you and I can go over to her together. I'm sure when she realizes it's all her fault, she'll . . ."

"But how can it be her fault?" Roy wanted to know.

"You *did* ask her if she colored her hair, didn't you?"

"Yes, of course I did."

"And what did she tell you?"

"She said, 'No,' it was natural . . ."

"And you believed her?" Paul asked.

"Well, I suppose so. But even if I didn't, what was I to do—call her a liar?"

Paul smiled. "Not in so many words, perhaps. Now, come on, let's get over there before she begins to feel a draft." By the time they reached the customer, there were several more curlers with hair on the floor. Luckily, Roy's "victim" turned out to be an exceptionally kind and reasonable woman. Initially, when she saw that Paul was going to help Roy, she seemed flattered by the extra attention.

She smiled at them and said, "Well, isn't this nice? When it comes to anything artistic, I always think two heads are better than one. Tell me, boys, will this be a collaborative effort?"

"No, dear," thought Paul, "this will be a last-ditch effort." Though if it didn't work, he feared, it would be more like assault and battery.

"No, Madam," he replied, "it's our policy to help each other whenever it's not too busy in the salon."

Gently, they began to remove what was left of the curlers from what was left of her hair. Then they began rinsing off her scalp, hoping in this way to neutralize the wrong permanent wave fluid Roy had used. They had to do this very carefully, for even a full head of hair is at its most fragile when wet. But even after they removed the remaining curlers, they knew they were in trouble. There were bald patches all over the customer's head, making her scalp look like a veritable patchwork quilt. Paul thought to himself that it would be perfect for tic-tac-toe, but then he caught Roy's nauseated look and warned himself to get serious and stay that way.

"You know, gentlemen, suddenly I have the strangest feeling," said the customer, her belated woman's intuition taking over, "like something's missing."

"The understatement of the year," thought Paul.

"Could I see a mirror, please?"

Paul thought, "The moment of truth," as they handed her a mirror and Roy made a face as if he were about to burst into tears.

She was, of course, horrified. She stared in shocked disbelief for a moment. Then she said, "Dear God!" and Paul guessed she must have been Catholic, for she proceeded to cross herself repeatedly, until she broke the long, red, beautifully manicured nail of her index finger. To keep her from adding the rest of her nails to the casualty list, along with her amputated curls, Paul took one of her hands gently in his and said, "You naughty girl! Why didn't you tell Mr. Tolliver here that you'd been bleaching your hair?"

She looked up at them, the expression in her eyes helpless and appealing. Paul felt some tremors of arousal, deciding that even if this one were totally bald, she would still be quite a number. "Oh, dear," she sighed, "I've been fooling people about that for years, and nothing like *this* ever happened before." She stared at her reflection again, and there was no denying how ghastly she looked, as if some carnivorous bird of prey had been tearing away at her scalp.

51

"Are you saying that even your hairdresser back home doesn't know?" Paul asked her.

"No, of course not," she said. "I didn't dare tell anyone. You see, my husband doesn't know I do artificial things to my hair, so I try my best to keep it a secret. This has always been something I do for myself, to keep him happy. But why is this happening to me now, of all times? I did so want to look my best on this cruise. You see, it's our tenth anniversary, and we've been having a kind of a second honeymoon."

Paul explained how she could have been spared this if she had told Roy the truth. As for the reason it hadn't happened before, Paul figured her own hairdresser must have been wise to her dyeing her hair from the start, and had acted accordingly.

"Oh, well, it seems I've only myself to blame," she sniffed, fighting hard to hold back tears. "I feel so stupid and ashamed. But how could I know what this little white lie would do to me?"

"Cheer up, Madam," soothed Paul. "It *will* grow back, you know. Besides, it could have been a lot worse."

"How?" she wanted to know.

"Well, look what happened to Pinocchio!"

Roy gave him a look of wild alarm. But, much to Paul's relief, the lady burst out laughing, tears mingled with her mirth. "Yes, you're perfectly right," she brightened, "at least my nose hasn't gotten any longer." She reached for some tissues and dabbed at her eyes. "Okay, gentlemen, tell me, how are you fixed for wigs?"

As it happened, they did keep a supply of wigs on hand for just this sort of emergency, but it was a very limited selection and many of them were just ready-made "fun wigs," hardly elegant enough for this classy lady.

What was worse, there were no blond wigs. The only suitable example was jet black. But they had no choice —

her natural hair looked an absolute fright. It took them two days to re-color the dark wig, after which they thinned it out and recut it so that it was fairly similar to her original hairdo. During those two days, she had to hide out inside her cabin. Although her husband was enraged when he first heard what had happened, his wife convinced him it was entirely her own fault for having lied about something so trivial, and he saw how pleased she was with the wig they had fashioned for her, so he agreed not to put Roy Tolliver on report. If that had happened, both Roy and Paul could well have lost their jobs.

In the meantime, Paul and Roy had gotten a chance to work together during this emergency. Even the rejuvenation of the black wig had been a joint effort. When it was all over, and Roy realized his job was no longer in jeopardy, he went to Paul and told him how grateful he was.

"I didn't deserve your help, as rotten as I've been to you. But you really saved the day for me, Barrington, and I won't soon forget it."

"Nonsense," said Paul. "I'm sure you'd do the same for me."

"No, you're wrong there. In the past, I wouldn't have." Then he smiled and offered Paul his hand. "But from now on, we're in this soup together." They shook hands on it, and at last the ice was broken. From then on, Paul included Roy whenever he and his other friends went to the ship's bar for drinks and conviviality, or into port to see what group mischief they could stir up.

In time, Roy confided in Paul about the heartbreak of his marriage. "You see, Terry and I did our training together, and I trusted her so completely for years. And, of course, I thought I knew her completely. There was nothing about her to make me suspect that she would . . . well, turn out the way she did. I mean to say, she was quite petite and feminine and sweet, and she used only the most refined, ladylike language. And now, it's as if I don't know whom to trust. I mean, if nobody's what they seem, where are you?"

"Look at it this way, Roy," said Paul. "The law of averages being what it is, don't you think it's highly unlikely you'd run into that kind of situation again?"

Roy thought about this. "Well, no, when you put it that way, I don't suppose it *is* the sort of thing that happens to everyone."

"Yes, that's exactly what I mean," said Paul. "What happened to you was like a freak accident, a once-in-a-lifetime thing. Mind you, I'm not saying you'll never meet another woman who'll betray you. But chances are, the next time that happens, she'll probably leave you for another man, not a woman." Then their eyes met and they burst out laughing together.

"Well, I must say, that's not a very bright future you're painting for me, Paul. Of course, I do see what you mean. We've got no guarantee we won't be hurt by people, no matter whom we trust."

"Right," said Paul. "But you've got to do it, trust people, I mean. Otherwise, you'll be stuck with no one but yourself, and that could get to be a very static proposition."

Roy nodded. "Then I'll simply have to take my chances and let myself get involved again. At least it'll be better than not feeling anything. That's the way things have been for me, you know, for a long time now."

"Good Lord," said Paul with a shudder, "the phrase 'not feeling anything' gives me the creeps, even to think about it. Me, I want to feel as much as I can, for as long as I can." Then he laughed. "In my spare time, of course, such as it is."

In the future, while it's true Roy Tolliver did let himself "get involved" again, it was in such a playful and promiscuous manner that it was clear he had lost all interest in another long-term commitment.

Not long after the ship left the Malayan port of Penang, Paul was permitted to see — and shave — his first live maharaja. If that had resulted in a simple, one-to-one relationship, it might have been an easier association. As it was, Paul also had to put up with the officious behavior of the maharaja's staff and security guards.

Earlier in the voyage, Captain Halprin had consulted with Mark Truesdale, asking him to line up his most proficient barber and keep him on call to shave the maharaja every morning during the remainder of the voyage to China. Although all the other hairstylists had received training as barbers, as it happened, Paul was the only employee who'd had some practical experience. As Paul put it when Mark asked him, "Well, I've shaved a dead Coldstream Guard in my time, so I figure a live maharaja should be a cinch."

When Mark recommended Paul, the captain said, "No, they insist only on the shop manager."

"But that's out of the question, Captain," said Mark, going fast into a panic. "I haven't shaved anyone in 20 years!"

"Oh, come now, Mark," said Halprin, "you shave yourself, don't you?"

"With an electric razor," said Mark. "If that will suffice for His Nibs, I'll be able to dust him off in no time."

"Nothing doing," said the captain. "I've been instructed by the company to give this VIP anything he wants, and he wants a close shave every morning by the shop manager. What's more, this has to take place one hour before the shop officially opens in the morning, so that the maharaja and his entourage are the only people in the shop."

"Then we'll simply have to convince them that Paul is the shop manager," said Mark, "because I promise you, Captain, if I'm the one to shave that silly potentate, his face will be a bloody mess by the time we dock in Hong Kong. That could well stir up an international incident, you know. But if you still want to try it, I'm willing to have a go at it."

The captain thought this over for a moment or two, then made his decision. If Paul was the only employee on hand when the maharaja arrived at the shop, he would naturally assume he was the manager. "That way he needn't ever find out we've deceived him," said the captain.

"But what do I do if he comes right out and asks me if I'm the manager?" asked Paul.

"Well, in that case you'd better be ready to lie, or else we could all be in trouble."

On the evening when the maharaja and his staff joined the ship in Penang, Paul had a glimpse of the band and the colorfully uniformed detachment of guards and well-wishers who had gathered at the dock for a send-off. The novelty of the occasion was like catnip for the hordes of inquisitive passengers who leaned over the *Chusan*'s rails on all the upper decks. Then, as the ship moved away from her berth, they could hear the strains of a very oddly rendered "Anchors Aweigh" from the band playing on the dock.

The next morning, Paul had to rush to get to the shop at seven, an hour earlier than usual. This would be the first time he had ever serviced anyone of royal blood, a fact that had kept him apprehensive and sleepless all night long.

He was only in the shop about three minutes when the door suddenly burst open, and there stood two enormous men in black suits. Startled, Paul wondered which one of them was the maharaja. He had half-expected the royal personage to wear something Asiatic, a toga or a turban, perhaps — and that, preceding his entrance, there might be a whole chorus of exotic dancing girls with rubies twinkling in their navels.

Not certain how to address these muscle-bound invaders, Paul began with, "Good morning, your royal . . ." but that was all he could get out. The men brushed past him, totally ignoring his existence as they proceeded to search the salon from top to bottom. They moved with amazing agility, considering their size. After they were satisfied that Paul was all alone in the shop and that, presumably, the place was devoid of all manner of explosives or other potential assassin's tools, they returned to flank the doorway.

No sooner were they in position when a small, neatly coifed older man strutted into the room. His face was thin, aquiline and birdlike—features that were accented by the small, peaked cap he wore. He was dressed in a woolen plaid dressing gown and slippers. This has to be Him, thought Paul.

"Good morning, sir," Paul greeted him.

The maharaja nodded and inquired, "You are the manager?"

Paul smiled charmingly. "Paul Barrington, sir, at your service."

He eyed Paul rather beadily for a moment. "So young to be so advanced," he said, speaking in perfect Oxford English.

"Oh, I'm not as young as I look, sir," Paul said, thinking if they demanded to see his passport, the jig was up.

Following the maharaja was his chief aide, another somberly dressed gentleman, carrying a briefcase. Presently the two bulky security guards bowed their heads, left the shop and quietly closed the door after themselves. No doubt to stand guard outside, thought Paul, with hand grenades at the ready.

When his esteemed patron got settled in his chair, Paul made sure he was comfortable. But as he started to lather the man's face, the aide moved a chair so close to his boss that he was planted right at Paul's elbow. That was bad enough, but not so bad as the sensation Paul got when he moved close to the maharaja and got a whiff of his breath.

My God, he thought, what did this little blighter have for breakfast this morning? Crushed monkey's brains in garlic? It was truly overpowering.

But those were the least of his problems. No sooner had his customer taken his seat than the sea suddenly started getting rough and choppy. This presented a new problem. While the barber chair was firmly fixed to the deck, Paul was most decidedly not. Consequently, the chair swayed with the movements of the ship, while Paul tried his damnedest to remain upright and not sway at all, especially since he would soon be brandishing a very sharp razor.

When he started to shave the man—very carefully, it must be noted—the razor missed its target with every other stroke, so that he ended up shaving nothing but air. It was like trying to shave someone on a bucking bronco. If only the maharaja had had a fatter face, something Paul could more readily set his sights on. As it was, the face was so thin, with so many nooks and crannies, it would have been difficult to shave standing still.

Paul's first few strokes down the side of the cheek went fine. But as his razor neared the chin, Paul encountered another obstacle: the maharaja wouldn't keep his mouth shut. He and the aide were in the midst of a heated business argument, yelling excitedly at each other in their own language. It was really getting to be a most untenable situation. The ship was swaying, Paul was terrified that he might soon spill royal blood all over the salon (in which case he was certain that the two Neanderthals waiting outside would come dashing in and clap him in irons), and he was also feeling a little queasy from combined effects of the royal stench of his customer's breath, the ship's rocking and rolling, and the loud, abrasive quarreling. Added to it all, he was beginning to get a headache.

The maharaja and the aide grew increasingly more animated in their debate and, finally, Paul put the razor aside and ceased operations. "I am sorry, sir, but if I continue to shave you under these conditions, I'm afraid I might do you a serious injury."

Both men fell silent and stared at him in wonder. It was as if they had forgotten he was present. "We are experiencing rough seas as it is, and that makes it difficult enough," Paul went on, "so, unless you keep your head and mouth very still and postpone your discussion until later, I will not take the risk of finishing you off." Even as he spoke, Paul wished he hadn't phrased that quite so clumsily.

"Finishing me off?" the maharaja said, giving Paul a cryptic grin.

"How dare you!" thundered the aide, rising to his full height. "Do you realize whose life you are threatening?"

"No, that's not true," gasped Paul. "I didn't mean that the way it sounded."

"Of course you didn't, old chap," said the maharaja, chuckling. "That's why it was so amusing." Then he turned to the aide and muttered something in his own language. When the aide made a half-hearted attempt to look amused, Paul figured his customer had just explained the joke. The maharaja then pointed to a far corner of the room, whereupon the aide took his briefcase there and stood with his back to them, gazing out through the porthole.

"Now, Mr. Shop Manager," said the maharaja, "you may proceed with your artistry, and I promise you that I shall not move a muscle."

"Thank you kindly, sir," Paul said. "I appreciate it."

Paul continued to shave this gentleman every morning, all the way from Malaya to Hong Kong. As if to keep his hand in, the aide insisted that Paul use an expensive new Kent shaving brush during each shave. He went on to explain his reasons for this extravagance, and Paul had quite a struggle to keep from laughing.

"We always take such precautions in order to keep our Beloved Ruler sterile."

After every shave, Paul handed the aide the "used" shaving brush, and watched as the devoted flunky opened the porthole and threw the brush out into the sea.

On the day before they were due to dock in Hong Kong, after Paul had given the maharaja his last shave, a steward appeared in the shop with a small package addressed to the shop manager. Naturally, this was delivered to Mark. As yet, no one in the maharaja's party had offered to pay for each service when it was completed, though that had been the shop custom, so Paul had come to the conclusion that such VIPs were given a free ride on board P&O liners.

But a few moments after Mark opened the package, he called Paul over to him. Not only had their illustrious patron enclosed all the money he owed, there was also a beautiful gold watch, to which was attached a brief note addressed to Paul.

"Good Lord, what a tip!" said Mark, examining the bejewelled gift under the light. "Tell me, Paul, what does he say in the note?"

A bit dazed, Paul read the note aloud:

> I want to thank you for your superb service, Mr. Paul
> Barrington. Keep up the splendid work and I feel sure
> that one day you, too, will become shop manager.

Paul stared at Mark, dumbfounded. "I'll be damned!"

Mark started laughing. "Why, that crafty little monkey! He knew you were an impostor all along."

"Yes," said Paul, fondling the exquisite watch in astonishment, "and instead of having me beheaded for my deception, he gives me this bloomin' watch."

"Congratulations, Paul," said Mark. "You earned it. But need I add that the drinks will be on you tonight?"

This would be Paul's first brush with the inscrutable minds found in that part of the world, though by no means would it be his last.

SIX

Among the many social aspects of Paul's after-hours activities on board ship was the opportunity to meet a great variety of personalities, some of whom were very famous in a purely dignified way, but many others whose fame bordered more on the notorious. As a result, Paul and his fellow workers often found themselves rubbing elbows with movie stars, TV personalities, writers, bank executives, and on one memorable occasion, even a flashy show girl traveling with her "sugar daddy."

Like old Harry Beaumont and his vivacious show girl-type wife, Denise. At least they called themselves "Mister and Missus," though Paul rather doubted their connection was a legal one. Harry was a rheumy old codger in his seventies, while Denise couldn't have been more than twenty-six. Paul had first met Denise in the salon, while doing her hair. From then on, she insisted that no one but Paul would even be allowed to touch her hair. She was so decisive about this that, one day while Paul was enjoying an afternoon off, Denise had actually tracked him down while he was having a much-needed siesta in his cabin. While she was sunning herself around the pool that day, her husband had gotten playful and had pushed her into the water, totaling the elaborate coiffure Paul had created for her for the dance that night.

The girl stood there in her two-piece swimsuit, looking much too curvy and tempting, at a moment when Paul was half awake and wearing nothing but his Jockey shorts underneath his robe. When he finally got around to viewing her from the neck up, he said, "My God, what happened to your hair?"

"Harry just tried to drown me, the old fool! Let me in, Paul, so you can put it back the way it was. Otherwise, I'll look like a wreck at the dance tonight!"

She started to edge her way into his cozy cabin, and he quickly said, "Meet me in the shop in about 15 minutes, Mrs. Beaumont. We . . . can't do it here."

"Okay," she said, scurrying away. "But hurry!"

When she was gone, Paul breathed a deep sigh of relief. We can't do it here, indeed, he thought, knowing perfectly well how much he had wanted to. Already he was beginning to understand the sort of frustration sailors had to contend with on long voyages.

Aside from seeing Denise Beaumont in the shop, Paul also ran into her with her husband a few times, in the restaurant or in one of the bars. Although they would be leaving the ship in Hong Kong to make connections for an extended round-the-world cruise, as a couple, those two made a lasting impression on Paul.

For one thing, they both spoke so loudly that you could hear them all over the dining room. For some unfathomable reason, Denise found (or pretended to find) hilarious everything her husband said. "Oh, Harry," she would squeal, "you positively kill me!" Then, to everyone within hearing range, she would add, "Harry used to be on the stage. He was one of the first performers to do a minstrel version of *King Lear* in blackface. Then he won $300,000 on the Irish Sweepstakes, retired, and proposed to *me*, all in *that* order. Ain't love grand, when you're in show biz?"

"That's what killed vaudeville!" roared Harry—a phrase he was to repeat with deadly monotony all the way to Hong Kong. His phrasing was usually accompanied by a seizure of laughter that left him gasping. Denise told Paul her husband was suffering from a chronic bronchial condition.

If that were true, Paul strongly doubted that the old man's health would be greatly improved by a vacation with rambunctious Denise.

On that last evening before they were due to dock in Hong Kong, Paul, Roy, Denny, and Jason were having nightcaps in the main cocktail lounge. Then, quite unceremoniously, Denise joined them, without Harry.

She took a stool at the bar next to Paul and, without a preamble, she proceeded to entertain the gentlemen with a collection of ribald (a better word for it would be filthy) stories fresh from the gutter. Not that her punch lines weren't hilarious, in a gross sort of way, but, since her voice carried all over the lounge, Paul noticed how nervous the others were becoming in being seen "fraternizing" with a passenger in such an intimate manner.

It wasn't too surprising that the chief purser was the first to take his leave. Then, one by one, the other guys also drifted off. Denise kept Paul on the scene by insisting that she needed his advice about a very personal hair problem. She was appealing to his professional sense of duty.

When they were alone, Paul said, "I think your hair looks perfect the way we've got it now, Mrs. Beaumont."

"Don't be so stuffy, Paul," she giggled. "What makes you think I'm talking about the hair on top of my head?"

"Oh?"

"You are a barber as well as a hairdresser, right?"

"Yes . . ."

"Then, if you've never had any experience using a 'Lady Schick' before, maybe I can be your first. I get so tired of having to shave myself down there, but Harry does prefer it to be as smooth as glass . . ." Suddenly, she stopped talking and stared at him. "My God, Paul, you're blushing! That's so cute . . ."

Paul attempted to laugh this off while trying to recollect his shattered poise. He said, "I think the lady has had a bit too much bubbly. Surely your husband must be wondering where you are."

"Oh, come *on*, Paul, I put that old gas hound to sleep an hour ago. Christ, you'd think a guy who's been guzzlin' booze for half a century would learn how to hold it. Not my Harry! He drinks like an old lady." Then she laughed. "Come to think of it, that's just about how he does everything. Know what I mean?" She gave him a nudge. Paul wondered if she were leading to something special, just between the two of them, and, if so, why wasn't he running in the opposite direction . . . fast?

"I'm gonna let him flop in bed 'til it's time for us to leave the ship in the morning," she said. "I gave him his usual cocktail of phenobarbital and bourbon. Works like a charm."

Paul eyed her warily, thinking that cocktail didn't sound like the perfect medication for a 75-year-old bronchial case.

"Anyway, with him dead to the world, it'll give me the first chance I've had on this voyage to find a little action of my own. I guess it isn't any news to you that my husband is a few decades older then I am."

Paul said nothing to this, eyeing her voluptuous blond reflection in the bar mirror, as he quietly sipped his drink. Could he believe these signals she was giving him? And, even if he did, was he crazy, to be considering such a fall from grace?

"I'm counting on you to help me out, Paul," she continued. "I'm getting claustrophobic lying alongside that snoring old basket-case every night, unloved and unwanted."

"Now, I'm sure you don't believe that . . ."

"No," she insisted, "I'm not kiddin'. I'm nothing more to him than a fancy ornament to show off to the tourists. In private, he doesn't have any use for me at all. But I think you know exactly what I want, Paul. And, confidentially, tonight's the night."

Paul had a vague idea it wasn't a wash and a set she was angling for. And now, quite suddenly, he could almost feel sorry for the poor, neglected girl. Imagine, a woman this lovely, married to someone who no longer had any need of her charms! And charms they certainly were, both of them! At this point in the voyage, it had been quite a while since Paul had had himself a nice, lusty weekend romp, due mainly to company rules about not fraternizing with passengers.

He turned and looked at her, thinking how appetizing and seductive she was, sitting there, fairly bursting at the bodice with girlish good health and hunger. Dare he let himself stray from the fold, just this once? Who would know about it? Here was his chance to have a girl who'd actually been on the stage. Only as a stripper, no doubt, he thought. But even that would be a big "first" for him.

Finally, he made his decision. He would give the little lady what she craved. He turned and delivered her a rakish smile, then (sounding *just* like David Niven) chanted, "Whatever you've got in mind, Denise, I think I can *more* than deliver. All you've got to do is whistle."

She didn't whistle. But, with a giggle, she leaned close and whispered in his ear: "There's a very young, Latin-type waiter who works in this bar, though I think tonight's his night off. His name is Alonzo. To me, he is just the sweetest hunk of stuff, you dig where I'm coming from? I've had my eyes on that cutie for days now. Tell you what, Paul—you fix me up with that beauty tonight, and I promise you won't *believe* the size of the check I'll give you in the morning!"

Paul nearly fell off his bar stool, to say nothing of taking a nose dive off his pumped-up ego. It's not *me* she wants, he thought. No! The tramp—she just wants a romp in the hay with one of the waiters, and she had me staked out as her flesh merchant! He couldn't believe what she had tried to make out of him. Beyond question, there was only one word for it, and the word was *Pimp!* Now, when he looked at her, he saw her for the cheap, deceitful adultress she was. And to think, out of the goodness of his heart, he'd been ready to take pity on her tonight and give her some comfort! He thought of her sweet old husband, so trusting and unsuspecting, lying asleep in his cabin. What a slut she was, he thought, without morals or redeeming social value.

Despite his anger, however, he couldn't let her see that he'd taken it for granted it was him she was hot for.

"My dear Mrs. Beaumont," he began sweetly, "when I hung out my shingle a few years ago, all it had printed on it were the words, 'Barber' and 'Hairdresser.' So, I'm afraid I'd be hopelessly out of my depth if I tried to 'double in brass' in quite the way you're suggesting. And, in case you didn't know, it's also against the law."

She was furious. "Well, get you!" she spit at him through clenched teeth. "Pardon me for living, Mister High-and-Mighty, I mean, *My God!* How stuffy can *we* get? What are you—some kind of monk, or something?"

Paul said no more. He simply hopped off the bar stool, gave her a parting smile, and said, "Now, Mrs. Beaumont, I bid you good night and good hunting."

But even as he left the bar, he heard Denise making lewd overtures to the young assistant bartender, who had a Latin look to him, but was in reality a wild-eyed young Turk. "Hi there, cute stuff," she said. "What're you doing after this joint closes, and how much do you charge?"

Tramp! thought Paul, quickening his step to get out of earshot.

But, as it turned out, that wouldn't be his last encounter with Denise Beaumont, or her husband.

At about five the next morning, Paul awoke to a frantic pounding on his cabin door. Jesus God, he thought, we've struck an iceberg! No—that would be impossible in this part

KENNETH PEARCE

of the world. Then he heard a woman yelling out in the
corridor, the voice both familiar and hysterical.

"Oh, Paul, I'm in trouble!" Drowsily, Paul grabbed his
robe and opened the door. There stood Denise Beaumont,
fully dressed. "Please . . . you've got to come with me, to
my stateroom, right away!"

"What's the matter," Paul mumbled, only half-awake,
"didn't the Turk work out?"

"Forget about that—it's Harry, my husband! He's had a
fall, and he's unconscious! Jesus, don't just stand there . . .
come on!"

Coming to life, Paul quickly asked for her stateroom
number. "What do you need that for?" she wailed.

"So I can give it to the ship's doctor when I phone him
right now," said Paul, going to the phone. "You seem to be
very confused about my occupation, Mrs. Beaumont, but
let me reiterate: I am a hairdresser, period, which means I
am neither a pimp nor a physician!"

It took a few minutes for him to arouse the very sleepy
Dr. Albertson by phone, but when Paul explained the emergency, Albertson snapped to attention and said he would
be on his way. "He'll meet you there," Paul told her.

"Oh, please come with me, Paul," she said. "I don't want
to go back there alone."

Jesus! he thought, how did I get myself into this? I left
her to her own devices earlier tonight, and she's still got me
involved! By the time he made it up to the first class cabins,
Dr. Albertson, also in his robe, was already on the scene.
Several passengers, just rising for an early morning jog on
deck, wandered curiously down the hall when they saw the
excited little group.

"Oh, Doctor, I'm so glad you're here," said Denise. "He
looked so awful when I left him and I was so frightened, I
didn't know who to turn to."

67

The doctor was eyeing Paul in surprise. "Barrington?" he said.

"Yes, Doc," said Paul smoothly. "I'm a—a friend of the family."

"Oh, I see," said Dr. Albertson, though it was clear he was both confused and distracted by the early-morning emergency.

When they opened Beaumont's door, they saw his inert body sprawled out on the floor by the bed. Although there were no signs of blood, the old man's face looked very white and pallid.

"I just came back to the cabin and found him like that, Doc," said Denise. Then, when she saw the others standing curiously in the doorway, she added, "You see, I couldn't sleep, so I went out for a long stroll on deck." Paul winced, as she wore a very flimsy and low-cut evening gown at the moment, with no sign of a wrap to keep out the cooling night breezes. "Harry was sleeping soundly in the bed when I left him, but look at him now . . . !"

They waited as Dr. Albertson went in and bent over the dilapidated vaudevillian. He placed his hand on Harry's throat, then reached into his bag for a stethoscope and listened for a heartbeat. Finally, he looked up at Denise.

"I'm so sorry," he said, "it's too late."

Denise gaped at him. "You mean, he's dead?"

"May God rest his soul!" said an old lady standing in the corridor.

"The poor man," said her companion. "To drop dead—on his vacation . . . !"

"I can't believe it," said Denise. "Any minute, now, I expect him to jump up and say, 'That's what killed vaudeville!'"

Once again, Paul felt a wave of sympathy for this girl, though, at the same time, he had to wonder what she had found so special with that young Turk that had kept her so fully occupied until 5 a.m. And all the while, her husband lay dying!

Quietly, the doctor approached the cabin door and asked the bystanders to disperse. Then he closed the door.

Denise said, "I guess I kind of knew he was dead as soon as I came into this room. But I couldn't face it alone. That's why I ran straight to Paul's cabin."

Paul again felt the doctor's inquiring eyes resting on him, though he managed not to return the older man's probing stare. But he felt sure the doctor was wondering how the hell this lady knew where his cabin was.

"Did he hit his head, Doctor?" Denise asked. "Is that what killed him?"

Dr. Albertson bent over the dead man again and examined him more thoroughly. "No, I would say this man has had a massive coronary. But surely, you must have known this, Mrs. Beaumont—a man his age, traveling with such a heart? You must have had him under special medication— like nitroglycerine tablets, perhaps?"

She was staring at him in a daze. "What nitroglycerine?" she asked. "And what heart problem?" She seemed truly astonished. "You mean, *that's* what he died of? But he told me it was a bronchial condition, I *swear* it! He told me that's what gave him all those chest pains and the shortage of breath, though sometimes his left arm would pain him, too, and I kind of wondered about that. Oh, hell, I've only known Harry a coupla' months, Doc, so I guess there's a lot he didn't tell me . . ."

Paul remembered what she had told him at the bar, about giving Harry phenobarbital and bourbon to help him sleep. Then, very quickly, he tried to shake those awful suspicions from his mind. If it were true that she hadn't known about his heart, giving him those pills and letting him drink to excess could have been a perfectly innocent gesture. On the other hand, to be absolutely sure of that, they'd have to know how many pills she'd been giving him, and for how long.

He exchanged a quick and intense glance with the doctor, and wondered if his suspicions had also been aroused. But Paul felt it would be best if neither of them voiced such suspicions. These people were ticketed to leave the ship in a few hours, anyway, so it wasn't the P&O Line's obligation to have the Hong Kong police search this lady's medicine chest. Nor was there any reason why they should let this incident create an unsavory scandal while they were aboard the *Chusan*. Let the authorities and the coroners dig up all those motives *after* the ship sailed on. If there were even a hint that a murder had been committed during the voyage, there was no telling how long the ship would be detained when they docked at Hong Kong. Paul clearly saw his duty: it was to the ship, provided Dr. Albertson didn't take any action. He could well imagine the repercussions if they had to hold up progress while waiting for an autopsy.

Besides, if Denise had been slowly poisoning her husband with a nightly pill, it was none of his affair. Just as certainly, he hadn't been the pimp she had taken him for earlier, and he had no intention to be a shipboard Sherlock Holmes.

"I'm so sorry, Mrs. Beaumont," said the doctor. "I suppose this will curtail the rest of your travel plans."

"No—actually, it will only end Harry's plans, not mine. I'll make arrangements to have his body shipped back to the States alone. You see, Harry wanted it that way. In fact, he told me so just a few days ago. He said to me, 'Denise, sugar, if anything happens to me on this trip, I want you to go on and finish our dream, just as I planned it.' So I think I owe him that much, at least."

The two men stared at her, Paul unable to believe that any woman could be this callous in such a situation.

"But what will you do about the funeral?" asked Dr. Albertson. "I mean, it will be several weeks before you're home again."

"So, they'll put him on ice for a month," she said. "Or, better still, I could always have him cremated." Here she actually laughed. "Sure, why not? That way, I'd only have to pay to have his ashes hauled."

Good God! thought Paul, as he watched the doctor's mouth fall open. If her feeble attempt to make a joke was a part of the shock and hysteria she was feeling, it might be understandable. But at the moment, he rather doubted this lady was feeling anything but relief.

"Actually," she went on, "sending anything air freight can really set you back these days and, if it was just his ashes, I wouldn't even need a box. An old brandy bottle would do it, or even a cigarette case. And I know just the one. It was a gift from Harry when we got married. Incidentally, you guys, this was supposed to be our honeymoon. Ain't that a kick in the head?"

With that, Paul decided it was a toss-up as to what had killed poor Harry: either the honeymoon, or the pills—both of which were inspired by Denise. No wonder she'd had to draft an emergency recruit last night. Somewhere between London and Hong Kong, Harry Beaumont had succumbed to a terminal expenditure of hormones, which could well have made this morning's heart attack a mere formality.

But, once again, if this lady *was* a cold-blooded murderess, Paul could only feel grateful that this would soon be Hong Kong's problem, not the ship's.

"Well, then, Mrs. Beaumont," said the doctor, "you haven't left me very much to say, except to wish you Godspeed with the Hong Kong morticians."

"Meanwhile, what do I do with the body?"

"I'll have two orderlies come up as soon as possible to transfer your husband to the morgue."

He went out the cabin door and disappeared down the hall as swiftly as he could, leaving the door open for Paul to make his getaway.

"Good night, Mrs. Beaumont," Paul said curtly. "I hope you enjoy the rest of your trip."

"Hey, Paul, wait a minute!" she said. "I think I'd feel kind of nervous, staying alone in this cabin now. Why don't I bunk in with you for a little nap?" She flashed him a lascivious grin. "This could be your last chance to get lucky."

He turned and glared at her. "Lucky? Are you kidding? I wouldn't even want to do your hair again, much less go to bed with you." She started to laugh, building up to a slow but, nonetheless, delirious crescendo. "But I'll tell you something, lady, the next time I get the urge to bed down with a black widow spider, you'll be the first one I'll get in touch with."

As he raced out of her cabin and down the hall, Paul could still hear her riotous laughter ringing in his ears. But one thing was for sure, he thought—until the orderlies arrived and took her husband down to the morgue, Denise Beaumont was all alone with her handiwork. It was just Denise and her dead meal ticket.

Paul didn't envy her those moments, not one bit.

SEVEN

More than anything, and despite the unlikely chance that he might run into Denise Beaumont, Paul looked forward to his first visit to the fascinating port of Hong Kong. During the ensuing years, this would become his all-time favorite city, with perhaps only Rio de Janeiro running a close second. As an international free port, this thriving island, he had been told, had the citified color and the rural peace of Old China, combined with all the conveniences of the modern world. And, since it was a British Crown Colony, it boasted a population of almost as many Europeans as Orientals.

His first view of that spectacular harbor was breathtaking and panoramic to behold. Never had he encountered such a diverse mixture of sights and colors. In one sweeping glance, he could see the many multicolored apartment blocks that sprang up from the precipitous green-and-brown hillsides, while beneath them spread a mile-wide strip of silver-green water, floating an extraordinary collection of vessels: an incongruous medley of bright-varnished company launches, cargo ships of a score of nations, police and customs patrol boats, the grimy motorized water-taxis called "Walla-Wallas," high-pooped fishing junks, little sampans poled by women with their babies nodding in slings on their backs, and self-important ferryboats dodging among the moored freighters and American warships.

The natural beauty of this harbor would have the same audacious impact on Paul no matter how often he visited it in the future. He saw it as a landfall made all the more dramatic because Hong Kong's New York-style skyline rises steeply on either side of a strait one to six miles wide. The two sides of the densely packed metropolis, hemmed in by its backdrop of hills, are today joined by a mile-long tunnel road, Asia's longest.

Hong Kong's northern side is called Kowloon ("Nine Dragons") because it was built on nine hills, at the tip of a small peninsula jutting out from the southeast mainland of China. It occupies only three and a quarter square miles, but to its immediate north, starting at Boundary Street, lie the New Territories, 370.5 square miles of mountainous land that the Colony of Hong Kong holds on a 99-year lease from China (soon to be called in). On the opposite side of the harbor is Victoria—originally Queen's Town—an intensely developed administrative and commercial center, clinging to the north shore of Hong Kong Island. The Island's rumpled topography assures that Victoria's "satellite" communities, like the Port of Aberdeen on the South Side, enjoy an insularity of their own, though they're in easy driving distance from the metropolitan area.

Beyond the dividing strait, to the east and west, the Colony also has 235 islands, mostly too small or too barren for habitation. Like jade carvings, they are strewn on the silky surface of the South China Sea.

Yet there is much more than location to make Hong Kong so breathtaking. Almost half of its four million inhabitants come from elsewhere, seeking economic or political freedom, and many, with good reason, do not consider themselves permanent residents. Hong Kong is the world's only major metropolis with a built-in time fuse, a "self-destruct" mechanism set to explode in 1997 when the lease on the New Territories expires and nine-tenths of the Colony reverts to China.

In this unique city-port, East and West are intermixed to an unrivaled degree. Here, two disparate ideologies coexist in a burgeoning cosmopolis that combines the magic and mystery and color of the Orient with the wonders of the technological age. Indeed, that there is a Hong Kong at all is something of a miracle. There are 404 square miles of land in the Colony, but, because of the hills and the mountains, 80 percent of it is not usable for either farming or building. The city has hardly any natural resources, not even sufficient food and water. Only dogged perseverance could enable four million people to live and prosper here. Their greatest achievement has been the transformation of Hong Kong from a shopping center — probably the biggest and most garish in the world, selling primarily other people's goods — into a booming manufacturing complex.

During some of his advance research, Paul had learned that, a century-and-a-half ago, Hong Kong was no more than a sleepy harbor: "Fragrant Harbor," as the Chinese had called it, a part of the Chinese province of Kwangtung. But Royal Navy Captain Charles Eliot, Great Britain's Superintendent of Trade for China, saw its potential. He had chosen Hong Kong as Britain's commercial and naval base when the Chinese were pressed to cede land to Britain at the close of the Opium War of 1839-42. Kowloon and Stonecutters Island were ceded in 1860, after another armed confrontation between the British and the Chinese. Eliot's sound judgment earned him the sack. Lord Palmerston, then British Foreign Secretary, censured Eliot for his "stupidity" in allowing the Manchu government to palm off "a barren island with hardly a house upon it." Young Queen Victoria, just four years on the throne, recorded how husband Albert had been "so much amused" by this utterly trivial addition to her overseas possessions.

It was, perhaps, a natural enough reaction. At that time, the island was chiefly a haven for pirates and opium smugglers, and had fewer than 6,000 inhabitants. Moreover, it lacked sufficient drinking water to support a population of more than a few tens of thousands. Even when typhoons delivered much needed water into the reservoirs, there was a heavy price to pay in death and destruction. The climate, except for three months of the year, was either hot and humid or cold and dank. Worst of all, malaria, cholera, typhoid, and bubonic plague regularly visited the poor fishermen who lived there.

Typhoons still roar out of the South China Sea between June and September. But disease has been conquered, level areas for housing have been created by land reclamation projects, and big new reservoirs have been constructed to provide adequate drinking water. More than a million people now live on Palmerston's "barren island," and another two million crowd Kowloon, a noisy hive of workers and pleasure-seekers that is crammed with shops, bars, brothels, clubs, factories, skyscrapers, and shabby tenements festooned with laundry. Sections of Kowloon enjoy the dubious distinction of housing the world's densest populations, with more than 300,000 inhabitants per square mile.

For days, crewmen had been warning Paul not to leave the ship in Hong Kong, saying he could be murdered, kidnaped, tortured, or all three.

"I've even heard stories of British crewmen being drugged and sold into slavery in this part of the world, Paul," Jason Rutledge had warned him. "You see, what they do is get you hooked on opium. Then they sell your ass to some visiting Arab or Hindu prince, 'cause those guys are as hot for boys as they are for girls."

"Oh, really?" said Paul. "Then I guess that explains why you're so eager to go ashore."

Jason laughed. "No, it's just that I can handle myself. I'm no greenhorn like you. Besides, I've got someone special I see when I'm in this city."

"Your own private Hong Kong stock, eh?" Paul teased. "Well, for your sake, I do hope she's a good girl."

"Hell, no, she's not 'good,'" Jason said. "But she's clean. And in this part of the world, that is one big distinction."

It was close to the dinner hour by the time they docked, and since most of the other guys already had their own "contacts" here, Paul at first decided to wait until the morning before going sightseeing, since he'd be doing it on his own. But when he saw that most of the passengers and crewmen were preparing to go ashore that evening, he quickly changed his mind. Besides, Jason's talk of having someone "special" had gotten him feeling both restless and horny, not to mention the "near miss" of his near-involvement with Denise Beaumont. She had turned on in him a lot of desire that he hadn't yet been able to turn off. Now, here he was in Hong Kong, that mecca of sin and danger, so didn't it figure he'd be ripe for an adventure?

Thus, Paul decided he would live dangerously that night. He left the ship and visited the notorious Wanchai district of Hong Kong. He told none of his shipboard pals of his plan, for fear they would try to scare him out of it. He strolled along that teeming waterfront, feeling a delicious sense of evil and intrigue as he passed one sleazy dive after another. He couldn't help but notice the bevy of beautiful young Chinese girls cruising the streets in their revealing *cheongsams*, or serving as tempting and provocative barkers in front of each bar.

Mustering up a large head of fool's courage, Paul entered one of the bars, and ordered a Gin Sling. But one small sip of that heady concoction told him it was much too potent for anyone who drank as sparingly as he. He placed the glass back on the bar. Then he glanced about the crowded place and tried to act as if he understood every language being spoken, though he couldn't make out a single word of English. What he heard mostly was a singsong smattering of separate Oriental dialects.

Suddenly, an exquisite young Chinese girl came up to him and actually spoke in English, such as it was.

"Hi, Charlie, you buy me dlink?"

Paul turned and eyed her closely, figuring she couldn't be a minute over 16. She was so well put together, he felt more intoxicated by her perfumed nearness than by the Gin Sling.

"Certainly, I'll buy you a *dlink* . . . uh, I mean a drink," he said. "But the name is Paul, not Charlie."

To this, she merely said, "Scotch and soda," which told him she hadn't understood a word he had said. He ordered the drink for her, but declined to have another for himself. When her drink arrived, she smiled at him, sipped some, then cuddled very close to him.

Naturally, Paul knew what line of business she was in. That naive, he could never be. In his present state of lonely frustration, he knew there was only one thing that kept him from taking her on for a fast therapeutic tussle — this girl looked like a one-way ticket to VD City, and he didn't happen to be carrying any penicillin on him.

"You likee me?" she asked him.

Paul nodded and smiled at her.

"You likee tits?"

That's one he hadn't been ready for. He found himself staring down into the valley of her cleavage and nodding his head and, as she nudged even closer, he had a feeling he wouldn't be able to walk out of there with any sense of propriety, not if his visible erection came along with him.

Then, when he remembered she didn't understand much English, he decided to speak that language fluently, thinking it might be a way to render himself unexcited. "I find you a very tempting morsel, my dear. But, you see, I want to make it back to my ship in one piece, and of all the souvenirs I had hoped to bring back with me, the clap was not among them."

She smiled at this, then continued her one-way conversation. "You be good to me, I make you happy, jus' like downtown." Giggling, she put her hand on his thigh and let her fingers do the walking, up, up and away, until Paul grabbed her little hand, though not before she had struck ground zero and let out a delightfully surprised, "Ooh, Charlie!"

Fearing that his growing excitement would soon become a public scandal, Paul took her crotch-bound hand in his, got to his feet and said, "Let's dance."

Luckily, the juke box was playing some American pop music at the time and Paul figured this way, he would be able to hold the little darling in his arms and still remain uncontaminated. He was reasonably certain you couldn't catch anything venereal simply by dancing. On the other hand, if the girl happened to have body lice, that would be another story.

While they danced, she looked up and gave him a sweet, virginal smile. "Fifty Hong Kong dollar I go all night with you, okay?"

Paul just smiled in reply, thinking that if he spent all night with this little firecracker, he'd have to put his glands in traction for the rest of the voyage.

At that point, a noisy mob of sailors and marines entered the bar. It took them only a few minutes of trading insults and obscenities before the conflict got very physical and the actual fighting began. Before anyone knew what was happening, chairs and tables started flying through the air. Paul made a nose dive for the floor, hoping to duck the flying furniture. The girl he'd been dancing with only a moment before had melted into the woodwork.

Paul tried to stand up just once when, in that instant, a sailor knocked a burly marine in the gut, knocking the guy against Paul and sending them both sprawling across the floor. After that, he didn't even try to get up. Not wanting to spend the rest of the voyage in sick bay, he wanted no part of this donnybrook.

Finally, he managed to crawl out to the street. But it was impossible to find a cab, and he was afraid to engage the services of one of the evil-eyed rickshaw runners. Due to Jason's warnings about being drugged and sold into slavery, Paul didn't know where the hell he'd end up if he trusted one of those denizens. So he ended up walking all the way back to the ship, and walking very fast indeed.

They were docked in Hong Kong for four days during that trip and, on the fourth day, Paul and his buddies were getting a little bored with the monotony and with the limited choices of the guys who wanted sexual *divertissement* without the threat of a lasting and traumatic infection. The more seasoned Hong Kong visitors like Jason, John Derringer, and even Dr. Albertson, who was a portly and conservative widower in his late fifties, appeared to have reliable "contacts" in port who were, as Mark Truesdale put it, "the germ-free kind of women whom one can bang with impunity."

For Paul and his co-workers, there was always a kind of enforced idleness whenever the ship was docked in port. At this time, customs officers came aboard and clamped their seals on the doors of all gift shops and salons, so no goods or services could be sold (otherwise these activities would be in direct competition with the thriving commerce of the local hucksters). On occasion, if the price was right, a customs officer might turn his back long enough for shop personnel to conduct a little under-the-counter profit making, though this was more likely to occur in Bombay or Colombo than in duty-free Hong Kong.

After a day or two of more or less conventional sightseeing with Mark, Roy, and Denny, Paul and the others still had some time to kill before they were due to sail on to Japan.

To while away that last afternoon, Denny came up with a slightly wild and definitely half-baked idea.

"Hey, you guys, let's do us a little fishing while we're sitting around, killing time. I hear these waters are infested with sharks."

Since none of them had ever fished before, including Denny, the fact that he wanted to go after sharks seemed like a lot of crazy fun. They didn't seriously expect to catch anything, especially since their only fishing gear was a long, heavy butcher's chain and a hook, which they baited with a large chunk of meat. When they got this together, about six of them threw additional chunks of raw meat off the lower deck into the harbor, to chum the water. They all had an idea that, with beginners' luck, they *might* catch something, though certainly nothing so major as a shark.

Then, it happened. A lively, outraged 14-foot monster snapped at their bait and proceeded to get caught on their makeshift hook, unable to shake itself free, no matter how vigorously it thrashed around against the side of the ship. "Holy bleedin' shit!" screamed Denny. "We've got us a real maneater!"

"Hold on hard, everybody!" yelled Roy. "And somebody call for reserves. It's either him . . . or us!"

"My God, I don't believe it!" cried Mark. "It looks absolutely furious. And hungry!"

"Fit to be tied," added Paul, "though I, for one, wouldn't want to be the one who has to tie it."

"What do we do with it if we catch it?" asked Roy.

"There's only one answer to that question," said Mark. "We don't catch it. We just let it go."

"No! We'll lose the butcher's chain," said Denny, "and it'll be our hides." And by now, there were a lot of cheering spectators, spurring them on to victory.

It seemed so idiotic. They had only gone fishing for a lark, and now they were about to catch a shark. Or were they? After enlisting some emergency help, they kept pulling and tugging until finally, they had actually hauled the flapping monster onto the deck. One of the crewmen, a man who could think on his feet, brought a gun and shot the beast to keep it from chomping on a few arms or legs before it breathed its last.

Then nearly a dozen of them just stood there in awe, staring down at their catch. "What a beautiful, accidental adventure," observed Paul. "Now I know a little of what Hemingway must have felt when he wrote *The Old Man and the Sea . . .*"

On those all too prophetic words, old Captain Halprin came descending upon them, more enraged than the shark.

"You goddamned lunatics!" he roared. "How dare you use my beautiful vessel as a common fishing boat!"

"Oh, boy," groaned Jason, "here it comes."

"Look, Captain," said Jason's aide, John, "we didn't set out to do this. It was . . . like an act of God!"

"There are long streaks of shark's blood running down the side of my ship," fumed the captain. "You call that an act of God . . . ?"

"Oh, no!" cried Mark. They all ran to the side of the deck and looked down. "Oh, Jesus," wailed a crewman, "that fucker really had himself a hemorrhage, didn't he?" Their flawless white luxury liner was now splattered with blood, from the waterline all the way up to the gunwales. "That'll wash off in no time, Captain," said Mark.

"Sure it will," steamed Halprin, "but not until I employ the services of several of my crewmen, who will now have to work their asses off until we sail in the morning, while the rest of you have been doing absolutely nothing since we got into port. Meanwhile, your orders are to get rid of that stinking fish, on the double, before they get a whiff of it up in first class." With that, he stormed off the scene, not waiting for any of their ifs, ands, or buts.

In the end, they had no alternative but to give the shark to the locals who would chop it up into pieces and take it home. But first, they remembered to take pictures of their catch to make sure the folks back home would believe the fantasy when the men spoke of it in the future.

EIGHT

Early the next morning, they were bound for Yokohama, Japan, a brief and leisurely voyage for most of the passengers, but for Paul and his colleagues in the shop, it was a nonstop marathon of work. It amounted to a four-day buildup of appointments made by lady passengers who said they much preferred to wait for the matchless expertise of the ship's hairdressing staff than to put their heads in the hands of the Hong Kong infidels, as one devoted fan of Paul's explained it. And thus, Paul discovered the real price of popularity — it was called nervous fatigue.

As they entered the Japanese port, Jason told Paul that he had better "latch onto one of those gorgeous little geisha girls before you succumb to cabin fever."

By now, Paul had grown used to Jason's affectionate kidding, for he knew this guy was ten years his senior and was much more worldly than he, having already been married and divorced twice. He also managed to juggle several hot and heavy, albeit discreet, affairs when he was in port long enough to get something going. Besides, Paul had already been warned about the dangers that might befall a novice in this part of the world, so he had promised himself to be cautious and not to let his potent sex drive rule his head — if possible.

"I want you to join me when we dock in Yokohama this morning, Paul," Jason invited him. "I think I'll take you with me to Chinatown, and see what we can dig up for you. Believe me, kid, with me as your guide, you can't go wrong."

When they got off the ship, Jason and Paul had a sumptuous lunch of Kobe steak and French fries, plus several slices of beefsteak tomatoes. Then they went shopping at the Kotomachi and Isezaki-cho shopping centers, which Paul found to be a delightful experience. But after that, Jason had something else in mind.

"Come along with me, pal; you're going to visit your first Japanese massage parlor!"

Jason accompanied this announcement with a lewd wink, so Paul knew he had every right to be suspicious. " 'Massage parlor,' indeed! So that's why you insisted on dressing up in civvies for this trip, Jason, instead of wearing your uniform. You want these girls to think you're a lot more than just a seaman!"

"Which I am, of course," said Jason. "But the less they know of my job status, the safer it will be, in case I screw up and do something else to shame the captain."

"Okay, what do we do first?"

"Find a cab," said Jason, which they did very quickly. "Incidentally, you're my guest on this trip, Paul, so I'll be footing the bills."

"Oh? Is it that expensive?"

"Well, first we have to pay to get in. Then there's the tip for the masseuse, and we'll probably end up having drinks and dinner."

"Then you'll be with me all the time?" asked Paul.

"Well, no, not at first. Mama-san will assign a young Japanese girl for you. And one for me."

"Okay, and what do I do first?"

"You take off your clothes."

"The hell I do!" said Paul. "Can't I at least have my Jockey shorts on?"

Jason laughed. "Sure, if you want to get them soaking wet when she gives you a bath . . ."

"Wait a minute, Jason. Who gives who a bath?"

"I do believe that's 'Who gives whom,' old chap," chuckled Jason. "But that's enough. I'm not telling you any more. I want you to be surprised."

"I'm surprised already, and we're not even there yet!"

Twenty minutes later, their cab pulled up to what looked to be a hotel. There were several signs on the outside, but they were all in Japanese, of course, so Paul was still in the dark. Jason led him to a small cagelike office in the lobby and produced several hundred yen. For this he received two tickets. He gave one to Paul, and together they went into the lounge and sat down.

In a few minutes, an elderly Japanese woman entered the room. She was made up like a geisha and dressed in traditional Japanese style. She bowed graciously and spoke in heavily-accented English.

"I am Mama-san. Pleased to have you in my humble place."

Paul and Jason stood and returned her bow.

Jason, who knew a little Japanese, said, "*Arigato gozaimasita, Mama-san.*"

The woman smiled at him. "You speakee Japanese, sir?" she asked.

"*Hai,*" Jason replied, meaning "yes."

It was then that a beautiful young girl entered the room. She wore nothing but a scanty two-piece playsuit, tight white shorts, and a mere strip of a bra. She was exquisite, a really delicious looking charmer. Paul judged her to be about seventeen and, since he was a few years older, he thought maybe he could treat her like a Dutch uncle, hoping she knew that young girls didn't go around undressing their Dutch uncles. Then, just when he was wondering what the hell he was doing there, she took him by the hand and led him out of the room.

Paul turned and gave Jason a last look of panic, but Jason just gave him a big grin and said, "*Banzai,* old buddy!"

The girl took Paul up a nearby stairway, and led him down a dimly-lit corridor. They passed several small rooms along the way. The doors were closed, but judging by some of the sounds he heard, Paul knew they were occupied, though if any of the occupants was getting a massage, it was certainly driving him to heights of breathless ecstasy.

When they arrived at the girl's room, Paul saw that it had no window. No view, he thought, which meant they couldn't look anywhere but at each other. The girl knelt down and began to remove his shoes. Then she bowed and said, "Please come in, honorable sir."

As he entered the small, hot room, Paul wondered exactly how "honorable" he was going to remain with all his clothes off?

"Please to undress, sir," she said.

Paul wanted to say, "You go first," but he feared she wouldn't understand he was joking. And maybe he wouldn't be. However, when he started to get out of his clothes, he was rather relieved that she had busied herself preparing his bath and didn't simply stand there and stare at him.

Finally, he had every stitch off and stood there, totally naked. Though he knew how silly it must have looked, he carefully folded both hands over his unmentionables. He didn't know which would be more embarrassing, if she giggled to see him hiding himself like that, or if she didn't start giggling until he took his hands away. If she did the latter, he decided he would never be able to hold his head up again, nor anything else, for that matter.

Never had Paul felt so foolish or so ridiculously frightened. And why not? Certainly, this was a premier occurrence for him. Here he was, about to be given a bath by a 17-year-old Japanese girl to whom he had just been introduced. Not that it would have been easier to take if he had known her all his life. This was certainly a far cry from his rakish weekends of liberty when he was with the RAF.

When the girl turned from the small bathtub, Paul saw it was only large enough for him to sit up in. Ah, but first, she had other plans for him. "Please to sit down on stool, sir," she said. "I will wash you before you take bath."

Why? Paul wondered. To keep from getting the water dirty? This seemed like a strange custom: to draw a bath, then do all the washing before you got into it. In any case, Paul was tired of standing on ceremony in the nude, so he sat down on the stool.

Then, without warning, the girl poured some very hot water over him.

Paul gasped, shuddered, and jumped to his feet, wondering what the Japanese word was for "ouch," and, in his panic, also took his hands away from his lower extremities. But the girl just smiled and bowed, as if to assure him that boiling him alive was not on the agenda. So he sat down again, a bit too hard as it turned out, because this time, he said "Ouch!" in English. Not being accustomed to sitting down naked, he had nudged both baubles before he realized he didn't have the full support he was used to. Lord, this is madness! he thought. A fellow could render himself incapacitated before he even finds out what's about to happen to him, if anything!

Now she started to wash his back with soap and hot water. Paul felt so nervous, he longed to be able to speak to her in a language she could understand but, at the moment, all he remembered in Japanese was *sayonara*.

After washing his chest, arms, and belly, the girl smiled and pointed upwards. Now, she wants me to fly, he thought. But she said, "Please to stand up, sir." He did.

She proceeded to wash his buttocks. Then, she came around to the front to take care of the rest of his decor. Except that Paul's major set piece did a lot more than just hang there. Even though he closed his eyes and bit his underlip to keep it from happening, old Mother Nature got a hold of his wherewithal and it rose, involuntarily.

At this point, the girl was squatting down before him and, when she saw his blooming accident, sure enough, she giggled. Not exactly a vote of approval, of course, though it didn't stop it from growing. Upwardly mobile and "damn the torpedoes," thought Paul. He was determined to accept no responsibility for what was going on down there. To act nonchalant, and perhaps even to reverse his state of arousal, Paul started whistling his country's national anthem, "God Save the King." Then, to his surprise, she also started whistling. When he recognized the tune, he was even more amazed. It was an old American ditty called "If You Knew Suzy." Hmmm, he thought, the Yanks have been here before me.

Then — and again without warning — the girl stopped all that whistling and threw a pail of ice-cold water on him. Taken by surprise once more, all Paul could do was jump and shout, somehow managing to convey to the girl that he was less than enchanted with her shock treatment methods and, at the same time, inadvertently deflating his outstretched member.

At last, he got into the tub, relieved that the member which was most vulnerable — and also most unpredictable — was no longer visible. But, after 15 minutes in that hot tub, Paul had really worked up a sweat. If he stayed any longer, he feared steam would start coming out of his ears, so he indicated to the girl that he'd had enough.

She helped him out, dried him off, then led him to a long massage table and told him to lie down on his stomach, which he did. Paul felt this would be a chance for a welcome rest. And it would have been, it the girl hadn't seized this opportunity to walk all over him, literally.

First, she straddled herself on Paul's back and began to massage him. That much he had expected. But a few moments later, he saw that she was about to climb onto the table.

"Where are you going, O pretty maid?" he queried. And then he knew, when he felt the pounding patter of her little feet stomping on his back. He vaguely recalled that this was supposed to be a world-famous erotic technique, though he also couldn't help wondering how something that hurt so much could also help.

He was just about to throw her off his back when the nimble little sprite sprang to the floor of her own accord. Then she deftly rolled him over on his back so she could continue her massage as a frontal assault. When she got down to the basics again, Paul revealed new evidence that they were indeed in the Land of the Rising Sun (though, astrologically speaking, and judging by her wide-eyed stare, he supposed the Big Dipper would be more like it).

She stopped massaging long enough to give him a meaningful smile. "You wantee special treatment?"

"Here it comes," he thought, "fringe benefits." But when she indicated what she had in mind (a Japanese hand job), Paul said, "No, thanks!" Then he held out his hands for her, "You see here? I've got two hands of my own, and they are both in perfect working condition. What else have you got on the menu?" With that, she smiled and offered simply, "Cost more."

"Okay," he said, and she began to get out of her halter and shorts. One look at the enticing goodies she'd been veiling convinced Paul that the time had arrived for him to take his libido out of dry dock. She was truly a gem to behold. Besides, he figured he had gone to all this trouble so, he might as well get something he couldn't do for himself. Hell, he had been giving himself a bath all his life, and certainly nobody ever had to help him play with himself. God knows that's what you *had* to do at sea when there were no other alternatives. But with a pretty little alternative like this on hand, he'd be a fool not to accept what she was offering. Or, to put it more philosophically, as someone very famous once said, "Man cannot live by bed alone."

This time, when she climbed back up on the table with him, she let Paul do all the walking, though first he was very careful to lay all the necessary groundwork. The longer that took, the better she seemed to enjoy it. He found it an added delight that she didn't attempt to rush him. Instead, she let him have two for the price of one, and Paul thought that was sporting of her, to give him a little encore on the house. When it was over with, he had to admit it had been both a relaxing and purging experience.

When he returned to the lounge, he saw Jason sitting there waiting for him, a knowing smirk on his face.

"Well, Paul, how did you like it?"

"You mean the massage? I found it very stimulating."

Jason eyed him shrewdly. "Come on now, you mean nothing else happened?"

Paul smiled. "To answer that question, my friend, I shall have to quote that old sage, Confucius."

"Oh yeah? Okay, so quote."

"Confucius say that some Orientals are not so 'inscrewtable' after all."

Jason laughed wildly. "And I'll bet you didn't read that in any fortune cookie, either. Now come on, let's go out and get gassed . . . !"

Later that night, by the time they were ready to take the bum boat (the ferry) back to the ship docked out in Tokyo Bay, both men were feeling quite merry, though a better word to describe Jason's condition would be "soused." As they stood out there waiting on the pier, there were several elegantly dressed passengers also waiting for the ferry. When the ferry arrived, Jason drunkenly decided that he would be the first to step aboard.

"Follow your leader, everybody!" he waved behind at the others. That's when he lost his balance, missed his footing, and grabbed onto one of the passengers to steady himself. This happened to be a lady dressed in a thousand-dollar ball gown and a diamond tiara. As Jason grabbed onto her, she grabbed onto her husband, and all three of them ended up in the drink, linked together.

Poor Jason! He had chosen one of the richest and most influential couples on the ship to half-drown. When they were all finally fished back onto the pier, Jason whispered to Paul, "Don't tell anybody I'm the purser. Or else Captain Halprin'll have my ass in a sling for sure!"

Amazingly enough, the woman didn't lose her tiara, but she did lose a pair of expensive, and much needed, eyeglasses. "They were custom-made just for me," she wailed. "They were Harlequins."

"That's funny," giggled a *very* merry Paul, "so are *we* . . ."

"But you don't understand," said her husband. "My wife can hardly see without those glasses."

"Then we're in luck," Jason whispered to Paul. "She won't be able to identify us."

The woman's husband was eyeing them suspiciously.

"You men aren't part of the ship's personnel, are you?"

"He is," said Jason pointing at Paul, "but I'm not." Since he had worn his civilian clothes that night, he managed to get away with this. On the other hand, the lady passenger had recognized Paul as her pet hairstylist long before she had lost her glasses; and since Paul hadn't been the one to give her the surprise soaking, Jason later told him it was okay if she knew who *he* was.

Happily, the couple had been fished out of the bay so quickly that no real harm had been done, except to their dignity and their wardrobe. During the rest of the voyage, that little dunking debacle did an instant replay in Paul's mind every time he saw this elegant lady being led around the ship by her husband. Without him to guide her, she might easily have gone around bumping into walls and people, or she could well have fallen overboard if her mate had looked away at the wrong time.

"Poor old thing," Jason said. "She's gone blind as a bat. Oh well, maybe they can buy a seeing-eye dog for her when we dock in Manila."

NINE

During the final day of their four-day stopover in Japan, Paul decided to visit the picturesque little town of Kamakura, which was only a half-hour's train ride from Yokohama. However, though he had reason to know he would encounter a language barrier in this part of the world, he had forgotten to go to Jason's office for the appropriate pass with directions translated in Japanese. For instance, Kamakura was the home of the great, giant "Daibutsu" Buddha, so the pass Paul would have gotten from the purser's office would have read, "Take me to your Buddha." Or words to that effect.

Instead, Paul found himself wandering all over that little town quite aimlessly, hating to admit he was lost in such unfamiliar surroundings. And certainly a blond Caucasian who stood about six feet tall would stick out like the proverbial sore thumb in this country of the tiny bowing people. In other words, he was fairly sure he couldn't pass as one of the natives, so his only hope was to find someone who spoke a little English.

The picture brightened somewhat when he finally remembered an old adage, or perhaps it was an old Boy Scout motto: "When lost, go in one straight direction so as to avoid retracing your steps." How long he should go in this direction was another question. For all he knew, this advice might take him straight to Outer Mongolia. On the other hand, he knew that if he wanted to get back to Yokohama, he would have to catch a train, so he headed for what he hoped would be the railroad tracks.

This trip took him down some very quaint, narrow streets where he observed the natives wearing colorful Japanese clothes—the men in long black kimonos, the ladies in their traditional, geisha-like kimonos—clopping along the street in their platformed wooden shoes. It was another half hour before he approached the railroad tracks, where he saw many taxicabs lined up in front of the station. Since he still had several hours before he had to return to the *Chusan*, he was still determined to find the famous Buddha.

Hoping one of the drivers spoke some English, Paul stood in front of one of the cabs and tried to describe the Buddha via sign language, plus a little rudimentary English. Something like, "Me want Buddha!"

He felt like an absolute fool when the driver smiled and said, "Oh, you'd like to go see the Buddha of Kamakura, wouldn't you?"

Dumbfounded, Paul simply nodded and got into the cab. When he stood in front of the famous idol twenty minutes later, he found the spectacular landmark so overwhelming, he knew it had been worth more than all his trouble to find it.

Built in A.D. 1252, the Buddha stood 42.5 feet high and had no fewer than 830 curls on its scalp, each curl about 9 inches long. Paul had read this earlier during extensive travel research, so he wasn't about to take his own personal inventory.

Luckily, he made it back to the ship that day with almost an hour to spare.

When they left Yokohama, their next ports of call were equally fascinating, since they were still Japanese. Paul again behaved like a wild-eyed tourist whenever he got the chance, in cities like Kobe, Osaka, Kyoto and Nara. Finally, the ship sailed into Nagasaki, where they were greeted by Japanese music and an array of festive balloons. Firecrackers were set off, too, to frighten away any evil spirits that might be on board, though Jason said he doubted very much if that would work on the captain.

Their next brief stop was Keelung, in Taiwan, which was (according to the current nautical scuttlebut) known as the "VD Supermarket" of the Orient—and for good reason, Paul learned when he discussed this with Dr. Albertson. Apparently, most of the prostitutes were the Oriental equivalent of what the West calls "juvenile delinquents," their ages ranging from 10 to 16.

"Girls of that age and illiteracy know nothing about the proper method of caring for themselves," the doctor told Paul. "And naturally, the unscrupulous people who exploit those kids don't care to get involved with the Health Department. In fact, these underworld types usually avoid officials of any kind. As a result, the strain of gonorrhea in Taiwan has become highly resistant to antibiotics."

For the most part, the disease was introduced by servicemen and merchant seamen from all over the world, though Paul later learned that the situation was even worse in Saigon. In that port, VD of every known variety had reached epidemic proportions.

When the *Chusan* finally headed toward the Philippines, the whole crew was suddenly in an uproar over a rumor that there was a stowaway on board.

"And this is no ordinary vagrant or bum," Jason said. As ship's purser, he was in a position to know the details. "In fact, she's gorgeous."

"She?" asked Paul.

"Right. She's an 18-year-old Japanese hooker, and the funny thing is, she's been on board ever since we left Yokohama."

"Hey," imagined Paul, "you don't suppose she could be the same one who . . ."

". . . Not a chance," Jason broke in. "You won't find this girl in any massage parlor. She's a high-priced call girl."

"Good Lord," exclaimed Paul, laughing. "Exactly what does she plan to do—set up shop among the crew?"

"No. She was smuggled aboard by one of her johns, some dirty, old, rich sugar daddy who was so hot to keep her on tap, he couldn't bear to part with her. I can't believe he's had her in his cabin ever since we left Yokohama."

"But how did you guys get wise to her?"

"It was the room steward who thought something suspicious might be going on, judging by the great amounts of food that old guy was ordering. He searched the cabin today while the guy was out. And he found *her* hiding in the bathroom, wearing nothing but a pair of panties." Jason laughed. "Little did he know what a reward he'd get for being so suspicious."

"Come on," admonished Paul. "You don't mean she offered him her body if he'd keep his mouth shut . . ."

"Something like that. Naturally, he told me he wouldn't hear of such a thing but, between you and me, I think he got a little before he turned her in. Hell, wouldn't you?"

"Hmmm . . ." Paul considered, recalling Dr. Albertson's recent VD sermons. "I don't think so. Not until I knew if she'd had all her shots. But what about the captain? Does he know?"

"He sure does. And tonight, when there's a kind of lull after the dinner hour, he wants me and some of my aides to stand guard outside the infirmary while the doctor gives this gal a smallpox vaccination."

"Before or after her blood test?"

"Whatever," shrugged Jason. "But she'll at least have to have the smallpox vaccine before we can dock in Manila. They're afraid that once all these horny seamen on board hear there's a young hooker on the ship, it may cause a riot. Who knows? They may break into the infirmary and drag her down to the engine room."

"But if that old fart who smuggled her aboard is so all-fired rich, why didn't he just buy her a ticket?" asked Paul.

"Well, he told me and the captain, too, that this little bimbo was damned expensive as it was. Apparently, she demanded a hundred bucks every time he put it to her!"

"Inflation," muttered Paul. "My God, it's everywhere!"

"And besides," added Jason, "she doesn't have a passport. Anyway, as it stands now, the old guy will pay for her ticket to Manila and back to Yokohama, so, under the circumstances, the captain says she can have a private room, with several guys standing guard outside."

"You think they may let her off the ship in Manila?"

"Why?" asked Jason.

"Well, by then I figure she won't have anything contagious, and . . . well, the day we dock in Manila happens to be my twenty-first birthday."

Jason stared at him. "No shit? Hey, does anyone else know about that?"

Paul grinned. "No, but they will now, since you're not exactly the type to keep a secret."

Jason laughed. "Yeah, well you can forget about this hooker. She's obviously bought and paid for. But don't worry, Paul. We'll dream up something special for you in Manila."

"Okay, but meanwhile, why can't I help you guys guard her outside the infirmary tonight? You said it would be after dinner, and I'll be free then."

Jason thought about this. "Yeah, I don't see why not. Should be fun, as long as you remember it's only a spectator sport."

"Sure, I understand," said Paul. "Audience participation is out."

By the time the girl arrived at the infirmary that evening, Paul, Roy, Denny, Jason, and his assistant, John, were all posted in the outer reception room. By now, the story of the stowaway whore had spread all over the ship and seemed to be of particular interest to the male personnel.

When Paul saw Dr. Albertson leading her through the reception room, he had to admit she was a luscious little baggage. Shiny black hair hanging down past her shoulders; full, pouty lips; and a lithe but very seductive body.

In passing, the girl winked at Paul and his pals, apparently deciding to do a little business. "Hi, Blondie," she smiled at Paul. "You likee fucky?"

Here we go again! thought Paul, though he was unable to suppress a chuckle as he said, "Well, that's not an easy question to answer."

"Don't give me bullshit," she snapped. "For you, I make it only fifty dollar. I like boys like you, tall, blond. You blond all over?"

Much to his embarrassment, Paul felt himself blushing. When Denny saw that, he got hysterical. "Hey, guys, look at his cheeks! My God, they're like apples!"

The girl started laughing, too. "No bullshit, baby," she said, winking at Paul. "You give me tleatment, I give you tleat! Is okay?"

But before Paul could answer, Dr. Albertson led her firmly into the infirmary.

Immediately, Paul and the others moved close to the connecting door, to hear the girl's conversation. It now sounded as if she meant to hustle the good doctor.

"Hi, Doc. You likee fucky?"

"Now really, my dear." Poor Albertson sounded flustered, though it was clear it was only because this offer was being made in the wrong place at the wrong time. The doctor had a reputation for never engineering an off-color dalliance while on board ship, though the guys wouldn't be surprised if he secretly arranged to meet her the next time he hit Yokohama.

"What's wrong, Doc?" the girl asked. "You likee boys maybe?"

"No!" Albertson burst out, and the guys had to stuff handkerchiefs in their mouths to keep from roaring at this. "It's just that this is no place for such talk."

"Okay," she said, "I come to your bed. Where is it?"

"We mustn't discuss things like this while we're on board this ship," the doctor explained. "So another time, another place. Now, relax and say, 'Ah . . .' "

"Ah, bullshit!" she fumed. "Why you talk so clazy? We don't gonna see each other no place but on this boat. How else we gonna do it?"

"I'm afraid that's the way of it," he said. "It just wasn't meant to be. Now please be quiet while I listen to your heart."

Suddenly they heard a commotion out in Nurse Joiner's office, which led directly to the reception room. A man was shouting loud and abusive language.

Jason ran to the door and threw it open. "What's going on out there, Jenny?"

At once, Jason recognized one of the ship's radio officers, a man by the name of Murchison who had a drinking problem and had been reprimanded severely more than once. At that moment, when he should have been in uniform and on duty, he stood there in civilian clothes, drunk and belligerent. By now, the doctor had come out of the treatment room and was glaring furiously at this intruder.

"Hey, Doc," slurred Murchison, "I hear there's a juicy little stowaway whore on this ship, and you've got her all to yourself in that treatment room back there. Think you're pretty smart, y'dirty old lecher? Whatsamatter, Pop, ain't you never heard of sharing the wealth . . . ?"

Before anyone expected anything more, Murchison bolted past the doctor and pushed his way into the treatment room. There he seized the girl, who was only draped in a sheet for examination. He tore off the sheet, slammed her down on the treatment table, started unzipping his pants, and fully intended to rape her on the spot.

To everyone's surprise, when the whore screamed, it was not because of fear, but in anger. She kept yelling, "NO! You pay me first! Money first . . . pay now, fuckee later! Get away . . . !"

After a moment's incredulity, Jason, Paul, and the others sprang to action. They hauled Murchison off the girl, though it took four of them to overpower him. The man was in a demented, drunken rage: "Goddammit, let me go! I'm gonna screw that little hooker just like everyone else on this ship!"

"You're dead wrong there, Murchison," said Paul, suddenly hitting on a bright idea. "Nobody on this ship would touch that girl with a ten-foot pole. She's got a case of the clap you wouldn't believe!"

Upon hearing the word "clap," the whore flew into a tantrum of her own. She sprang at Paul, her nails at the ready. "Big liar! I got no clap! Who tell you I got clap? I clean, like whistle! But now for *you*, I charge two hundred dollars!"

She was draped in the sheet again but, during this diversion, Murchison lurched away from his captors just long enough to snatch the sheet away and make a grab for her breasts. For an instant, the "guards" were so entranced at the sight of the nude young girl standing before them that they gaped in stupor, Denny crossing himself and blurting, "Holy Mary, look at those honeydews!"

"Don't just stand there, you leering idiots!" the doctor upbraided them. "Get that drunken slob out of here. And, Nurse Joiner, you take that girl into the other room at once!"

Jenny seized the girl, throwing the sheet over her again, after which she led her out of the treatment room, the whore now cursing all of them in Japanese.

Jason and his helpers headed for Murchison, blocking his way out of the room. "Wait a minute, men," instructed the doctor. "Since his pants are half-off anyway, pull them down completely so I can knock him out with a shot."

"Oh, no you don't!" Murchison yelled, and once again the fists started flying.

But, finally, they were able to hold him down, his jeans and briefs removed. The doctor gave him a strong sedative injection in his right buttock.

Within seconds Murchison calmed down, passed out, and thus one more oceangoing adventure was brought to an end.

On the *Chusan,* as well as on other P&O liners, it had become a much anticipated tradition to have a gala costume ball about mid-voyage. This was scheduled on the night before they were to dock in Manila. Paul and the other hairdressers had already done a great deal of advance preparation for this event. The ship's most seasoned lady passengers made elaborate plans for this occasion months ahead of time, having bought their costumes long before boarding the ship.

Weeks earlier, Mark Truesdale had told Paul about the woman who was going to the ball as Marie Antoinette. *"Before* she was beheaded, unfortunately," he'd added, "which means we've got to come up with an appropriate wig for her. She asked me if I had a hairdresser who might be interested in doing some historical hairstyling, and since I've been majoring mostly in the 'hysterical' variety of late, I thought of you. How about it? Care to have a shot at it?"

"Sure, why not?" Paul had replied. "Sounds like a great challenge."

The lady showed up for her appointment that afternoon and Paul was ready for her. During the voyage, he had devoted an hour a day to working on this cranial creation, for he literally had to build it from scratch. To create the base on which to plant the hairpiece, which would stand 22 inches above her head when completed, Paul used the cotton wool stuffing from an old chair nobody sat on anymore. It was in the officers' lounge and, when Paul saw that it was slowly coming apart, he would go in, casually sit down from time to time and pull out bits of stuffing, a little more each time. He also used chicken wire to help the wig retain its solidity. And to glue the hair together, he used glue made of sugar and water.

When his patron entered the salon that afternoon, Paul at last presented her with his finished masterpiece. She was a lovely blonde in her mid-thirties — tall, statuesque, and with such an enticing figure, Paul felt it would be a pity to camouflage all those curves within her period costume. This was none other than *the* Mrs. Derek Winslow, married to (though on the voyage not accompanied by) the seventh richest man in the world as stated in his biographical profile in Dunn & Bradstreet, circa 1951.

She arrived in full costume, having everything scheduled down to the last minute. Paul was to do her makeup as well as the wig, so it would be a four-hour production. When he presented her with the finished hairpiece, she seemed utterly enchanted.

"Oh, Paul, I'm just thrilled to pieces!" she exclaimed. When she showed her appreciation by throwing her arms around him and kissing him full on the mouth, Paul rather wished he could pick up some of those pieces. Lord, she was a stunner!

"I'm glad you're pleased, Mrs. Winslow," he said. "You really inspired me to come up with something special."

"And you certainly came through for me, darling, but please, no more 'Mrs. Winslow.' I'm Christine, and you're Paul. And because of you, tonight I'm going to be the belle of the ball and win first prize for most original costume. And darling, when that happens, I'll tell everybody that I owe it all to my hairdresser. Now, wipe that lipstick off your mouth and get to work!"

During that four-hour interim, while Paul did her face and hair, there was an abrupt change in the weather and the seas grew unexpectedly rough. For a while, it was touch-and-go whether or not to postpone the ball. Finally, when Captain Halprin got the latest weather report, he announced via the public address system that the weather would start to calm down by five that afternoon, ". . . and we should have ourselves a truly gala night!" Earlier that day, however, the seas had grown so choppy, lifelines had been strung up all over the ship on the outside decks to keep people from falling overboard if they lost their balance.

Paul spent so much time working on Christine Winslow's hair and makeup that he was late getting to his next appointment. But the next lady was so fascinated by watching him work, she didn't seem to mind the wait.

"Isn't he incredible?" asked Mrs. Winslow, when she realized the other client was so intent on watching the procedure.

"Oh, yes," said the lady in waiting. "Why, he's more like an architect than a hairstylist."

"Yes, I suppose," said Christine. "But I much prefer the word 'artist.' Of course, we shouldn't be saying all this in his presence. It's outrageous enough that he has all this talent and he's also handsome, and so young!"

Paul was used to this harmless flirting, though he had often wondered how many of these gilt-edged teasers would be willing to put their bodies where their mouths were, if he was crazy enough to call their bluffs. Not that he dared give it a try, of course, since it could well lead to an instant dismissal if the wrong person found out about it. Paul had already heard some horror stories about former employees who had not been able to resist temptation while in the line of duty. When the women looked like Christine Winslow,

105

and you happened to be a super-heterosexual hairdresser, there was always the risk that the sheer proximity of such perfumed fleshly contours might do you in.

Luckily, Paul was so intensely involved with his work that day that he managed to divert his mind from such fancies. Finally, his "Marie Antoinette" was complete. Paul wished her good luck, she gave him an effusive hug, and literally danced out of the salon.

Then, only a few moments later, came the disaster. It wasn't until later that night that Paul heard the grisly details of this tragedy.

When Mrs. Winslow left the salon, she had only an hour or so to kill before it would be time to make an appearance at the ball. As she was in full costume, which included her towering hairpiece, there was no chance for her to simply lie down for a bit of a nap. But she felt so warm in the costume, and the weight of the wig was threatening to give her a migraine. And, too, as the seas were still rather rough, she feared she might get seasick and upchuck all over her costume unless she got some fresh air.

"So, like a fool, I just did it," she told Paul later. "I threw caution to the winds and stepped out on deck."

She was only outside for a moment when a huge wave swept over the top deck and totally inundated what had, only seconds before, been an exquisite replica of Marie Antoinette. In a trice, Paul's historical hairpiece was riding the crest of a whitecap, no doubt to end up as shark bait. The next time he saw the lady, she burst through the door of the salon and just stood there, dripping and groaning.

Paul and his customer gaped at her in horror. She was a bedraggled mess, soaked to the skin, right down to her hair follicles. He was stunned. It couldn't have been more than three minutes since she'd left the shop, looking superb. And now, look at her, he thought. Instead of Marie Antoinette, she looked like the Creature from the Black Lagoon!

"My God, what am I to do?" she wailed. "I know I was silly, but I needed some fresh air . . . I was feeling queasy." It was a time to be frantic, since the festivities were due to start in about 45 minutes.

"You think it would help to put me under one of the dryers?" she asked, then answered her own question. "No, I guess not. Even if I dried all this mess, I'd still look like something from under a wet rock."

Finally, Mark and some of the other operators were drawn into the emergency. They all took turns staring at this human accident known as Christine Winslow. Mark kept shaking his head and saying, "It's impossible." And then, "Of course, if Marie Antoinette were known to wear a wind-blown bob, maybe we could fake it."

"Well, she looks a sight and no mistake," Denny said, unable to keep from giggling. "Like something that just came up from Davey Jones' locker."

With that, Mark pointed a finger at Denny and said, "That's it! Forget Marie Antoinette. The thing to do is to change your character and go as is."

"As is?" Christine stared at him. "But look at me! I've even got bits of seaweed in my hair, if you can call this hair."

"No, dear," Mark said, "that's perfect."

"You are quite mad, my dear fellow," she said. She looked at Paul. "Paul, tell him he's mad."

"I'm afraid I can't," said Paul. "He's my boss."

"Don't you really know what I'm trying to tell you?" said Mark. "First of all, you've got no time to be making any elaborate repairs. Okay, so it won't be a total loss, why not go as Mother Neptune?"

"Oh, good heavens, yes!" cried Christine, staring at herself in the mirror again. "Now that I already look like a half-drowned mermaid, why not use it? Yes, that just may be the most original touch of the evening."

They decided not to do a thing to her splattered hairdo. She went to her cabin, found an old nightgown, and they all helped her tatter it to shreds, after which they stuck a crown of seaweed around her head, and there she was! For her scepter or 'trident,' they found an old broom handle donated by the cruise director. With her hair as damp, wispy tendrils framed about her face, she looked as if she had just been swept up out of the sea, in time for the ball.

Denny was the only one with a dissenting opinion.

"I hope you know you've got this all wrong, according to ancient Greek mythology."

"What're you raving about, you silly Aussie?" demanded Mark.

"According to the books, Neptune was a god of the sea, which means he was a man."

"Oh, really?" said Mrs. Winslow. "Well, I have news for you, dear; he just had a sex change."

When she went on to win first prize for originality that night, Paul felt it was partly because she was such a good sport. Everyone had known for weeks how meticulously she had been planning for her triumph as Marie Antoinette. However, from where Paul was looking, the way her clinging sea-dress clung to the contours of her smashing figure, her sudden change of costume had been a decided improvement.

The next morning, when the ship was due to dock in Manila, Paul awoke, very curious, wondering what sort of "surprise" Jason had planned for his twenty-first birthday.

TEN

There would be a three-day stopover in Manila, but because that first day was Paul's birthday, Jason told him that he and some of his buddies had the whole day mapped out for Paul's entertainment. In their party would be Jason, his assistant, John Derringer, the chief Officer, Vladimir Pulaski (a native of Poland who spoke near-perfect English), Roy, Denny, Mark, plus the only two female employees brave enough to join this gang of hellbent males—Jenny Joiner, Doc Albertson's young nurse, and Madge Barton, one of the ship's switchboard operators. Madge was a pretty and vivacious brunette in her mid-twenties and although Paul didn't realize it until that little jaunt, she and his bitterly divorced co-worker, Roy Tolliver, had been engaged in a very surreptitious shipboard romance for some time now. Now, when Paul saw these two together, he realized they must have been on fairly intimate terms for some time, judging by the idolatrous looks Madge gave Roy without appearing to care very much who noticed. Assuming this was a genuine love match, Paul later found time to tell Roy how happy he was for him. "As long as you two don't get careless enough to drop your guard while on duty."

"Oh, come on, Paul," Roy had said jokingly. "Living dangerously is half the fun of a fling like this. You'd be surprised at some of the secret little places Madge finds for us to hump our troubles away. I swear, that girl's insatiable, and so inventive."

"Really?" Paul said, somewhat surprised by this cavalier attitude. "Then, apparently, it's not serious between you two. I was almost sure you were secretly engaged, or . . . or something."

"Engaged? You've got to be kidding. You don't think I'd want to marry a little curbstone free-for-all like Madge Barton, do you? No, indeed! This is just a little harmless bangathon, to break the monotony. You really ought to try it more often, Paul, and not only when you're ashore. Believe me, there are lots of ways to get your jollies in transit, if you're clever enough and discreet."

The term "bangathon" had so depressed Paul after that conversation that he vowed never to take such reckless chances while on board ship, no matter how sorely he might be tempted. But little did he know that in a few years' time he would be ready to eat those words, with considerable relish.

As for Jenny Joiner, she was a buxom lady in her early thirties, with fiery red hair and a temper to match, should any man get the wrong idea about the state of her morals. Jason told Paul she had once read him the Riot Act when he had tried to give her a "helping hand" in a manner she wasn't ready for. She told him she had signed up to be ship's nurse because she'd always had a wanderlust, adding that the kind of lust he had in mind did not appeal to her.

Jason didn't believe her, of course. "They all talk like that at first, until I let them get close enough to me to get hooked."

"And has this happened with Jenny as yet?"

"Well, we got close, but I'm afraid I'm the one who got hooked," said Jason, laughing. "Seems Jenny's ex-husband was an amateur boxer, and he taught her some moves I wasn't watching for. Man, what a right hook that gal's got! But I was lucky she was on hand when my nose started bleeding, as she took me to sick bay and treated me herself. But only as a nurse. So far, I haven't convinced her how much more she wants of me. Don't worry, though . . . I can tell what's on her mind every time she looks at me."

"Poor Jason," Paul had kidded him. "If only you had a little self-confidence."

After breakfast that morning, they all took a bus trip to Baguio, the famous summer resort. That was a harrowing drive over narrow, winding canyon roads. Up and up they went until they were about 5,000 feet above sea level. But the climb was well worth it when they turned around and saw that breathtaking view. On the way back, they passed many little *nepas* (houses) built with sliding walls of bamboo with shell windows. Everywhere they went, the natives waved and shouted a friendly greeting at them. Paul would soon learn that the average Polynesian disposition was very laid-back and tranquil, as if they had nothing in the world to worry them. Later that day, Jason had dreamed up a very festive dinner party for Paul in Manila. During this stopover, they were all staying at the stunning new Sheraton Philippines Hotel, and Jason, wanting to go all out for Paul's birthday, had grandly reserved a small banquet room for this little get-together.

By "dinner," Jason made it clear to his friends he was talking about the kind of food that was typically indigenous to the Philippines. "You know, gang, I've recently made a study of gourmet Polynesian foods," he told them, "and for this auspicious occasion, I think we should all 'go native,' if only in a purely culinary sense."

"Exactly how 'native' are we going?" Denny asked.

"Well, there's one special dish I've heard about here in the Philippines that I've been dying to try," Jason replied, "something called *balute.*"

"Yes, I've heard a lot about that one," said Mark, "though I've never tried it myself. It has quite a history, though. Apparently, due to its special nutritional powers, that delicacy helped save many lives during World War II, a time when there was precious little food available for the masses."

"Isn't that the stuff I hear them peddling on the streets here in Manila?" asked Jenny.

"Yeah, that's the stuff," said Chief Pulaski. "Especially late at night. That's when you can hear the *balute*-seller making his rounds, singing out his wares the way the old fruit peddlers used to do back in Poland."

Jason had engaged a local guide for this outing, a boy by the name of Armando who appeared to be half-Spanish and half just about everything else. Jason told the boy he planned an adventurous food-and-drink *soirée* for his friends, and that he wanted the star offering of the evening to be *balute*.

With that, the boy stared at him so strangely that, at first, Jason thought he had mispronounced the word.

"Sir, are you quite sure it's *balute* you want?"

Relieved to hear he'd pronounced it right, Jason said, "Of course I'm sure. Why? Are they hard to get?"

"No, no. I will have no trouble to get them. It is just that I wondered . . ." The boy eyed Jason closely again. "Have you eaten them before, and do you know what to do?"

Winking at the others, Jason said, "Naturally, I've eaten them before, and they're delicious. In fact, that's just how they were described in the gourmet guide book I read."

"Ah . . . the gourmet guide book," Armando repeated thoughtfully. Then he gave Jason an apologetic smile, apparently convinced that he was a seasoned devourer of the dish. "Then tell me please, how do you prefer them, eighteen days old or twenty days old?"

Jason stared at the boy, and felt his guests staring at him. Paul was wondering if this stuff didn't come any fresher than that but, not wanting to spoil Jason's "surprise," he curbed the impulse to ask that question.

"Oh, just use your own judgment," Jason finally said to the boy, trying to make his voice sound bored and nonchalant.

"And how about the wine?" asked Armando.

"Yeah, how about that?" Jason said.

"Would you like *Tuba* wine, or do you have some other preference?"

"Anything but Muscatel," Denny said.

"Now, come on, Armando," said Jason, bluffing it out. "You know as well as I do there's only one wine that's right for *balute.*"

Armando smiled. "Yes, of course. The *Tuba.*"

Then he hurried off to unearth their treasure.

"You know something, Jason," said Pulaski, "the kind of food you've been talking about sounds more like a language barrier than a menu."

"Right," said Denny, "that's what I was thinking. Here we're all about to eat something called *balute,* while we drink something called *Tuba,* and they both sound more like musical instruments than food."

"Hey, does that mean it'll sound like a real symphony when we all burp after dinner?" asked Mark.

"Oh, Mark, you *are* a silly one!" Madge gave him a little poke.

"Come on now, you people," said Paul, coming to Jason's defense. "Jason's taken great pains to plan all this, so where's your sense of adventure?"

"Well, I don't know about you," Denny said jokingly, "but I don't like to think of my stomach as a high-risk area."

"Well, naturally we'll let Jason try it first," said Jenny. "If he doesn't turn turquoise, that means it'll be safe for the rest of us."

"Thanks for that vote of confidence, cutie," Jason winked at her, "but I'll bet you dollars to doughnuts it'll be delicious."

"If it isn't," said Denny, "can we all have doughnuts?"

"Oh . . . shut up and whet your appetite!" laughed Jason. "But actually, according to my research, the *balute* is supposed to serve as *hors d'oeuvres.* There'll be a lot of other goodies on the menu afterwards."

Finally, Armando arrived with his exotic prize.

But they were surprised to see that the boy only carried two small bags in his hand. "And after all that advance publicity?" Paul wondered. Jason seemed equally surprised, though he presumed there was wine in one bag, while whatever the *balutes* were lay nestled mysteriously in the other. But if that was enough for nine people, it couldn't add up to more than a mouthful apiece. To save face, however, Jason pretended he knew just what was happening.

With great *savoir faire,* he proceeded to open both bags and place their contents on the cocktail table. There were eighteen *balutes* and four bottles of *Tuba* wine. Jason stared fixedly downward, pretending to be fully prepared for what his eyes and nose beheld.

Then he inhaled.

That was his first mistake. His nostrils were assailed by such an ungodly stench that his eyes began to water. His first thought was "There's something rotten in Manila!" But he was very proud of the implacable expression he kept on his face as he ogled what looked like eighteen hard-boiled rotten eggs.

"Twenty days old," he thought. "Hummm . . . one day older and they could have jumped off that table and formed their own union."

And, yet, it was the wine more than the *balutes* that won top award for air pollution at that little dinner party. One whiff of that brew and Jason was sure this would be the closest he'd ever come to germ warfare.

"Good God, Jason!" said Jenny. "What on earth *is* that stuff?" She and the others were looking about as enthusiastic as anyone can while holding their nose.

But Jason was equal to this challenge. With Armando watching his every move, he was proud of the way he carried this off, like a true epicurean. "This, my dear friends, is the fabulous *balute!* I have it on good authority that it's the most coveted dish in the South Pacific . . . "

". . . At the bottom of which is exactly where it smells like it belongs," said Denny. Ignoring this, Jason said, "And now, shall we all have a round of applause . . . ?"

". . . Then," Jason continued, "I shall pass among you . . ."

Denny and Mark exchanged a wild look and started laughing uproariously. "With a bed pan?" Denny inquired, between titters. "Now come on, you guys," Paul said, "let's be a little more sporting about this. Remember, Jason's doing all this for *my* birthday, and you don't hear me complaining!"

Jason grinned at him. "Now there you have it, folks," he said, pointing at Paul, "the meaning of true loyalty in a crisis."

"Now that's very commendable," said Chief Pulaski. "And if Paul here wants to eat a crisis for his birthday, it's up to him."

"Ah, sir," Armando said, addressing Paul. "Then this happy occasion is in *your* honor, yes?"

"Quite right," Paul said, giving the boy a smile. "It's my birthday. My twenty-first, actually."

"Then should you not be the first to sample this treat?" Armando suggested.

Jason jumped at this. "Armando, my lad, you just took the words right out of my mouth. He's right, Paul. It's only fitting that you should be the first tonight. You know, the rites of passage and all that. That way, you will never forget how you celebrated your twenty-first birthday."

"Oh, come on, Jason," said Mark. "This is beginning to sound more like some college initiation than a birthday."

"No, don't be silly, Mark," said Paul. "I like the idea. However, I do think it would be more festive if Armando here first showed me the proper way to eat this . . . uh . . .

delicacy. How about it, Armando, would you care to do the honors?"

The boy smiled at this, though Paul tried not to take note of the derisive gleam in his eye. Then he proceeded to demonstrate.

"You see, in reality, *balutes* are chicken eggs that are boiled just when they are about to hatch."

"Now *that's* festive," said Denny.

"If you will move in more closely," Armando entreated them, but no one did, "you will see that in some cases the head of the baby chick has begun to pop out of the shell before the egg was placed in the boiling water, so we have almost caught the very moment of birth and frozen it with fire. Then we let it sit for two or three weeks so it can gather flavor . . ."

"Uh huh," muttered Pulaski, "like sewage."

"Now, the proper way to eat *balutes,*" Armando continued, "is to knock the top of the egg off. Then drink the soup, which tastes very much like chicken broth, you know?"

"Now *that* I love," said Roy.

"Do you, honey?" Madge said, nestling closer to him. "Then someday remind me to learn how to cook."

". . . After that, you peel off the baby chick's feathers and then you eat it," said Armando, "bones and all."

"Well, of *course!*" said Mark.

"Afterwards, you wash it all down with *Tuba* wine. It is as simple as that."

"Sure it is," said Denny. "Then comes the autopsy and we go straight through probate."

Nothing more was said for a moment as they all stared expectantly at Paul, who realized they didn't want to reveal their revulsion in front of Armando which, he had to admit, was very thoughtful of them.

"Paul, I'll make a deal with you," said Jason. "If you're game enough to eat one of those things tonight, in honor of your birthday, so will I."

116

"Oh, Jason," said Jenny, "are you sure? I mean, wouldn't it be a little like eating a mother hen's abortion?"

"Don't get medical," Jason said.

"Besides," said Paul, "that's all in the mind."

"Not after we stick it in our mouths, it isn't!" she gave back.

"Well, frankly," Paul said bravely, "I don't believe in knocking anything I haven't tried." Then he glanced at Armando and saw the gleeful malice in his eyes, which told him there was only one thing he could do to convince Armando and the others what a daredevil he was prepared to be on this historical landmark of a night. My God, he thought. I'm twenty-one — that means I can vote and drink and . . . and eat *balutes!*

"Go ahead, Paul," Jason urged him. "You go first and I'll follow. We can think of ourselves as pioneers."

Suddenly, the others got in the spirit, even singing a refrain of "Happy Birthday to Paul" to let him know they were solidly behind him and that they'd be willing to try this smelly repast if *he* did. Which told him that maybe their olfactory nerves were getting used to the stink by now.

Nevertheless, thus inspired, Paul threw out his chest and took a deep breath. A bad move. By now, the whole room smelled like the bottom of a *very* neglected bird cage.

He took a good slug of the *Tuba* first, praying it might contain enough alcohol to anesthetize him for the remainder of the ritual. But after one swallow, he prayed the dead chicken's fetus would take away the awful taste of the wine.

Gingerly, he knocked off the top of the egg, which also flipped off the unborn baby-chick's head, making this seem a lot more like capital punishment than an *hors d'oeuvre.* But, at least, there'd be one less hunk of chicken flesh he would have to devour. Still determined to carry this off with a gallant flair, he seized the rest of the diminutive cadaver and began to de-feather it. Fast.

Out of the corner of his eye, he could see everyone staring at him, as if they were spectators of a play in which they had no intention of playing a part. A play called *Arsenic and Old Eggs,* what else? For a moment, Paul felt it would be a lot easier for him to hatch those eggs than it would be to eat them.

Finally, after saying a small prayer (something like God save my lower intestines), he popped the egg and the headless baby in his mouth and chewed up a storm. "Ugh!" said his palate to his digestive tract, while his brain tried to convince him he was really eating boiled chicken with a little egg salad on the side. But, when he washed that tangy excrement down with the vile-tasting wine, his brain gave up the struggle and admitted it was garbage.

Then he swallowed it all and heard a ringing in his ears, which did *not* sound like birthday chimes. But, good soldier that he was, he still managed to turn and take his bilious sideshow bow. "There now, you see, everybody? Once you get the knack of it, it's a real eating experience."

He stood there feeling both nauseated and proud of himself as they all applauded and cast their admiring eyes on him. When they were finished singing "For He's a Jolly Good Fellow," Paul said, "All right, now everybody line up, it's your turn. You go first, Jason."

"*Not on your life!*" they all sang out unanimously, including Jason.

Appalled, Paul couldn't believe his ears as he gaped at them and tried to hold his temper. What kind of sportsmanship was this? Armando, who had somehow managed to avoid tasting the stuff during his pompous explanation, now gave Paul a mischievous chuckle as he darted out of the room.

"Hey, you guys," Paul said to the others, "is this what I get for my birthday—mass treachery?"

"Look at it this way, Paul," said Jason. "In the future, when you talk about this—and you will, believe me—this night will live in the infamy of your memory like no other night ever will, not in your entire lifetime!"

"Hear, hear!" said the others.

"Bastards!" Paul said, wondering how he could be laughing and feeling so nauseated, all at once.

Once again, they sang "Happy Birthday to You" in Paul's honor, though this time they altered the lyrics to suit the occasion.

Denny began the refrain, and the others took it from him: "Happy Kaopectate to you, Happy Kaopectate to you," and so on.

However, despite the civil war being waged in his innards, Paul's evening was not a total loss. His guinea pig heroics taught his friends an important lesson when it came to ordering the rest of their dinner. They bypassed all the Polynesian dishes that Jason had suggested earlier and, instead, ordered good old reliables like steak or roast beef, cooked Caucasian style.

As for Paul? When his yummy birthday cake arrived, he dutifully blew out all the candles. For dinner, however, he ate sparingly: some medicinal beef broth, followed by a quick run to the facilities, whereupon he sneaked out later for a double Pepto-Bismol on the rocks.

ELEVEN

On a voyage that was already crowded with memorable experiences, the brief stopover in Bora Bora was another episode Paul would not soon forget. It was there, while he and Jason spent the day sightseeing, that he learned of the peculiar attitude the Polynesians had toward burying their dead. It seems that when one dies in Bora Bora, one has the right to be buried in whichever place one had the most fun in while one was alive.

"Think of that," said Jason. "What a way to turn all their whorehouses into funeral parlors!"

Paul laughed. "I don't think they have such places here. It's not that kind of culture."

"You mean everybody does it for love?"

"From what I've read, they rely a great deal on barter."

Because of this bizarre burial custom, there were no designated areas on the island such as "cemeteries." Instead, there were graves scattered in some of the most unlikely places — in the middle of a schoolyard, underneath a favorite tree, next to a bakery, or even near a favorite candy store. In most cases, it seemed that each family preferred to bury its dead in the front yard. The graves were covered over by a flat cement slab, which served as a kind of miniature playground for the children in the family. Apparently, it didn't bother the little tykes one bit to hop, skip, and jump all over the sealed-in remains of a relative. Thus, little girls would sit on these leveled-off tombs, happily playing with their dolls while, in other houses, people might use the cement slabs as a base for their garbage cans.

Perhaps, thought Paul, this was the Polynesian way of affirming that death was a part of life, and in this sense he found their attitude rather refreshing. At least they didn't have the strong aversion to their dead that prevailed in so-called civilized society (i.e., one great big barbaric ceremony, and then simply "file and forget," out of both sight and mind).

Their ensuing stop at Rarotonga, in the Cook Islands, was equally as interesting, though practically everyone on board agreed this had to be the most godawful sailing interlude of the whole trip. The weather was cold, squally, and windy, and the waves reached from ten to twenty feet.

"Did you ever get the feeling this is one very fickle ocean we're sailing on?" Paul asked one day while having lunch with Roy, Denny, and Mark. "When she's good, she's very, very good; but when she's naughty, she's really a bitch."

They laughed heartily at this. "Wait until you've been at it as long as I have, Paul," said Mark. "Then your language will be comprised entirely of four-letter words."

By now, Paul had become relatively immune to seasickness, so early the next morning he was one of the few people in shape to appreciate the gorgeous sunrise in the distance, with Rarotonga dimly visible on the horizon. In that quiet mood, he recalled the interesting old legend the natives had going for them. In Rarotonga, the old people believed that when you came to their island, the gods attached an elastic thread by one end to you, and the other to land. While you remained, you were not aware that this thread existed. Only when you left did you feel its first gentle urgings. With distance, the pull became ever greater, until one day you felt compelled to return to Rarotonga. It's like an umbilical cord, Paul decided. Though little did he know how relevant that thought would become a little later that same morning.

A young Japanese woman came into the shop to have her hair done. Although Paul had seen her once or twice before in the shop, he had never waited on her. She dressed in modern western garb, and wore her lustrous black hair in a shoulder-length bob. But she spoke only some very halting English. Now, for the first time, Paul noticed something about this lady that he hadn't observed before; she was unquestionably pregnant. So much so that she bulged out quite noticeably, despite the loose maternity garment she wore.

She was quite tiny, so perhaps that was why she looked much more pregnant than she was. From the look of her, Paul half expected her to pop over any minute, but he figured she must know her inner timetable better than he. When she noticed Paul's hesitancy, she smiled and said, "One more month, please. Not today." Then she put a hand over her tiny rosebud mouth and giggled. Not today, Paul thought, trying to giggle along with her to make her feel more comfortable.

When he realized she spoke little English and understood even less, he gave up trying to chat with her. She had indicated to him that she wanted, "Same way hair, only clean." Paul translated that as a wash and a set.

It was a bit awkward when he had to push her forward to extend her head over the sink during the shampoo. With the water running, he didn't hear her groans as a result of this action. And also, it was always rather noisy in the salon at this time of the morning. As he kept his hand against the nape of her neck to hold her steady for the wash, Paul whistled while he worked. Then he turned on the nozzle-shower to rinse off the shampoo, and it was then that two things started to happen. His customer began saying something unintelligible in Japanese, and Paul gasped when he felt water splashing all over his shirt and trousers.

Oh shit! he thought. "Mark!" he called loudly. "We've got a plumbing emergency over here. I think the pipes are leaking . . ."

Mark hurried over to them. One look at the customer, whom he recognized on sight, and at Paul's curiously drenched-looking trousers, and he knew the situation at once.

"Plumbing emergency, my ass!" he said. "This lady's water just broke!"

"Her water . . . did what?" Paul asked. Then he stared down at himself, and a few telltale whiffs told him the scented shampoo he'd just used did not smell like this. "Oh my God, and she said it wouldn't be for another month yet."

"You can forget that," said Mark. "When the water breaks, the baby's usually the next thing to come gushing forward."

"Gushing forward," Paul muttered. "You mean she's having a baby here and now?" This time his voice carried and suddenly the whole shop was in an uproar. Mark went to the phone and put through an emergency call to Dr. Albertson. Then he saw the cluster of alarmed and slightly half-baked looking lady customers circling about. Oh Lord, he thought, what'll we do until the doctor comes?

"Is there a midwife in the house?" he yelled, forgetting for the moment that none of these ladies' husbands earned less than a hundred thousand a year.

The expectant mother was now grunting and wailing in agony as she squatted in her seat. Paul removed the bib and tried desperately to make her more comfortable. He wracked his brain to think of helpful hints at a time like this, but the truth was that he had a very small frame of reference.

"She's having convulsions or something," said Denny. "I'm sure it's the same principle as when my Labrador retriever had her last litter back home. She kept grunting like she was tryin' to throw up but, after each grunt, out popped another pup. It's a bloody marvelous thing to watch!"

"Ask her how far apart the pains are," said one of the lady customers, her hair all foamed and reeking from a beer shampoo.

"We can't ask her anything," said Paul. "She speaks very little English. I think she's even moaning in Japanese."

"How do you say 'press down' in Japanese?" Mark asked.

Just then, the woman let out a scream that gave everyone a chill. But, thank God, Dr. Albertson came running into the shop only a minute later. As it turned out, he spoke fluent Japanese, and quickly asked Mark to put out a call for her husband. "Have him paged!"

While he examined her, the poor woman was actually pressing her feet against the sink, groaning and writhing in her seat. "Good God, she's in labor this very moment!" he told the others.

"You mean she's going to have her baby here, in the shop?" asked Mark. "There now, Paul, you see what you did? You're about to become a godfather."

"The trouble is I'm short of staff this morning," said Albertson. "It seems everybody's seasick, after that last bit of rough weather we came through. But not to worry, somehow I'll manage to get her to the infirmary." He reached down and lifted the groaning woman in his arms. She was drenched with sweat and fluids and water, soaking the doctor's pants the moment he took her in his arms. Then he told Mark to hold the door open, after which he hurried across the salon with his patient, and nearly collided with her hysterical husband.

"What you doing?" the frantic little man screamed. "Not baby yet. Not have it for one month, in Honolulu. We make plan."

"No, not one month," said Albertson. "Now! Don't you see, her water broke."

"Then you fix, okay? Make well."

Albertson shifted into Japanese again, and the little man looked as if he understood, though that didn't calm him down much. But suddenly the patient started screaming, this time in English. "Is coming . . . is coming . . . now, please, is coming . . . !"

"No, dear, not yet," said Albertson. "In just a few minutes we'll have you in the nice, clean infirmary, where you belong."

"No!" she screamed, having new convulsions in his arms, "is now, now!"

The doctor looked down at her, then stopped all further motion. "Dear God, she's right. We'll have to do it here . . ."

"No, my baby not come here, in shop," the woman's husband cried. "We lose face!"

"Get his face out of here," Albertson demanded of the others. "And someone unwind that barber chair over there, and hurry, please!"

But technically speaking, this blessed event happened before Albertson could reach the chair. As he rushed across the room, he heard the unmistakable cry of a newborn baby, arrogantly shoving its little body out of the womb almost of its own accord. He looked down and saw the tiny emerging head and shoulders and torso, all of it, sliding and oozing out into daylight. "Oh, Lord!" he cried, "she's doing it right in my arms. Never in my entire career has this ever happened to me. But hurry, now, flatten out that barber chair!"

Once he had her on the chair, and they drew a curtain around his area of operation, the doctor did the rest of the honors with only a minimum of help. The baby was a girl, all six pounds of her. Paul offered to fill in as the attending nurse.

Albertson looked at him. "Do you faint at the sight of blood?"

"No," said Paul, "just pus."

"Oh, that's lovely!"

"No, Doc, I swear, just tell me what to do," Paul insisted, "anything!"

"Okay, find a way to sterilize your scissors so we can cut the cord," he said, sweating profusely as he held the blood-splattered infant in his arms. "And get me more towels, somebody, please!"

After lighting a match under his scissors for a moment, Paul prayed that would do it. When he gave this to the doctor, Albertson, in turn, handed Paul something half-wrapped in a towel. "What's this?" Paul asked.

"The placenta," said Albertson. "Get rid of it."

Paul handed it to Mark, who passed it on to Denny, who looked as if he might keel over, until he handed the whole mess to one of the half-done customers.

In another few minutes, the doctor had the infant washed and toweled down, and had given the mother a sedative shot, though she was still alert enough to know what was going on. Now that they had all been able to witness this miracle at sea, Paul and his colleagues stood around and gazed at this tiny new passenger, each of them caught up in a feeling of awe and wonder.

"Isn't it astonishing?" asked Paul. "All I did was try to wash her hair, and she had a baby."

"That's all right, Paul," said Mark. "Nobody's blaming you. The culprit is lying over there." He pointed across the room where the father was being vigorously fanned and slapped by some hovering lady customers, for he had fainted dead away.

Later, the doctor came back and thanked everyone for their support in the emergency. He also said the young couple were so grateful, they named the baby after him.

"How about that? 'Suzuki Alberta Yamakawa.' Has a nice ring to it, don't you think? Of course, by rights, she should have added your name in there, too, Paul. I don't know what you did exactly, but as it turns out, you were the last human contact she had before she gave birth."

"Yes, isn't it lovely?" Paul said, a slightly beatific smile on his face. "Here, I've just turned twenty-one, and already I've gotten another man's wife in the family way. And I don't even speak the language."

"Oh, you've got the touch, all right," said Mark, "and no mistake."

"It's called 'the laying on of hands,'" said Roy.

"No, it's not," said Denny. "It's kismet, pure and simple." And so it was.

TWELVE

The remainder of Paul's first voyage on the *Chusan* proved to be comparatively smooth and happily free of emergencies, so by the time he did his brief layover in San Francisco, he decided he had come through the very worst "trial by fire" of his entire seagoing career.

Nothing he had heard about San Francisco had fully prepared him to be quite so bowled over by the scenic delights he found in that city. Actually, he had heard so much advance praise, he figured the reality could never live up to his expectations. But he was wrong.

Never in all his travels had any city so completely lived up to the promises made about it in the travel folders. Later, he would think of it as a tantalizing composite of Lisbon, Hong Kong, Acapulco, Copenhagen, with a touch of Sydney, Australia, for good measure. And yet the sum total of San Francisco was purely unique. It belonged exclusively to itself, like no other place in the world he would visit. All those hills and shifting views, with the very climate appearing to change its mind from one neighborhood to the next. It was a shimmering, iridescent kaleidoscope of towers, seascapes, and color.

*   *   *

During the next five years, Paul would never tire of the excitement of his experiences as ship's hairdresser. During his last eighteen months of service, he worked in the elevated capacity of shop manager; and though he would occasionally work with the same people from one voyage to the next, it wasn't always feasible to keep in touch with some of the good friends he had made on his first voyage. While he served on the *Chusan*, Jason Rutledge still worked as chief purser, so he and Paul could continue their friendship. But, in time, Paul worked on other P & O liners, like the *Canton* and the *Himalaya*, both of which were exact, and similarly luxurious, replicas of the *Chusan*. Roy and Denny shipped out with him from San Francisco, as did Mark. But during Paul's first voyage on the *Canton*, he had to start from scratch and make all new friends once more, as there wasn't a soul on board he'd ever laid eyes on before.

And yet, the challenge of meeting new people with new stories to tell never failed to excite him. True, on occasion there were some of his fellow workers who were impossible to befriend, no matter how willing or expansive he was. In time, he would come to miss Mark Truesdale and the mischievous Denny, both of whom eventually chose futures on dry land.

During his first voyage on the *Canton* in 1953, the ship took off from San Francisco down to Los Angeles. From there, they sailed along the coast of Mexico, docking briefly in tropical — but oh so humid! — Acapulco; then down to South America, stopping at several ports in Peru and Chile; across the South Pacific to Easter Island, Pitcairn Island, Tahiti; and from there to Fiji, New Zealand, Australia; and, finally, to Indochina, Asia, and the Near East.

The captain of this ship, a jolly giant of a man by the name of Joe Clarkson, was a warm, ingratiating character, which made him a refreshing departure from the rather officious regime Paul had experienced under the command of Captain Halprin. Unlike Halprin, Clarkson wasn't obsessed with the power of swinging his weight among his subordinates, nor was he the sort of guy to pull rank or stand on ceremony with his underlings.

Despite his awesome size — he weighed about 260 pounds and stood six feet six — he was very easy to be with and eager to communicate with all crew members, from the highest to the lowest. On that trip, Paul's good buddy was the chief steward, a young Londoner by the name of Warren Praeger. Whenever Paul and Warren got Captain Clarkson in one of his story-telling moods, sometimes over a drink in the bar, he would come up with a great variety of fascinating tales about his adventures at sea. The men could sit for hours, listening to the captain reminisce about his forty-plus years as a seaman. At the same time, Paul was more than just entertained — he also learned a great deal more about the science of navigation than he'd ever imagined he wanted to. Not that such information would be helpful in the ship's beauty parlor, but still, as a crew member, working under the ship's captain, he felt there were certain things he ought to know about what kept his floating home in operation.

As for Paul's myriad adventures ashore, these continued to be just as harrowing over the years. During a Mediterranean cruise on the *Himalaya* in early 1955, there was one three-day stopover in Morocco — particularly the teeming city of Tangier — that he would never forget. He would always see it as something of a miracle (or perhaps he should praise Allah?) that he ever got out of that city alive.

Paul and some of his buddies had planned their little excursion for weeks, knowing in advance how much time they would have. During this adventure, among his companions was the ship's assistant purser, Mel Goldstein, a native of Brooklyn, New York, whose accent Paul found almost as unintelligible as that of the cockneys at home. Then there were Ginny and Tina, two switchboard operators who, despite their overt femininity, only had eyes for each other.

Paul was still naive enough to be shocked when they told him the "score" between them. "Look at it this way, Paul," said Ginny, amused by his reaction. "Won't it be a relief for a gorgeous young guy like you to know he'll be absolutely safe in our company?"

"Hey, that's right," said Tina. "This way, the three of us could even sleep in the same bed together and you'd never have to fight us off."

Paul had already found them both charming as friends, even before he knew their secret, so he decided their sex life was their own business and he still wanted to see as much of them as ever. Not that he really wanted to be all that "safe" where women were concerned. Still, it was nice to know that either of these two pretty lasses might well try to cripple him via Judo if he ever so much as made a grab for a tit.

His pal, Mel Goldstein, was living evidence of this hazard. When Ginny said she'd break his arm if he made a pass at her, he didn't believe her. As a result, he walked around with his arm in a sling for two weeks. "I thought she was just handing me a line," he told Paul. "I mean, they both look so cuddly and soft and yummy; who expected them to come on like John Wayne?"

"Okay," said Paul, "that means we'll just treat them as friends."

"Yeah, I guess so. But shit, I've never had a pervert for a friend before. What the hell do we talk about?"

"Think of them as a couple of guys," said Paul. "You know, like us. What do we talk about mostly?"

"Sex. Or how long it's been since either of us scored."

"Well, maybe not that," Paul said. "Maybe we'll stick to sports and travel, since those two are clearly monogamous."

"Yeah? Is that what they call it now? Whatever happened to 'tutti-frutti'?"

"No," Paul laughed, "monogamous means they only have sex with each other. They're faithful."

"Faithful, my ass! It would only take one good crash course from me to show 'em what they've been missing."

"Don't try it, Mel. Unless you want them to break your other arm." Mel didn't try it.

And so, for their jaunt in Tangier, it was just the four of them, though Mel said this was definitely not the kind of "double date" he'd been dreaming about.

"You know, Paul, all my life I've wanted to ask some beautiful broad to 'come with me to the Casbah,' and now I end up with one broad who'll probably be inviting her girlfriend to do the same thing. Where the hell does that leave me?"

"Look, Mel, if you want someone to hold your hand in the Casbah, okay, I'll be there right alongside of you."

"Thanks a lot," Mel laughed. "That hard up I'll never be. Jesus, at least I hope not!"

They rented a secondhand station wagon for their sight-seeing trip. But they made a rather unfortunate first impression. Despite several advance warnings, Ginny and Tina forgot to hide their cameras from the natives. They had all been told it was forbidden to photograph a Muslim. Cameras scare the hell out of these people. They fear they have been robbed of their spirit, and it is against all their beliefs to be "duplicated" in any way, perhaps thinking that the photographer has despoiled the original.

So they were greeted with stones and rocks. Of course, to stone one's enemy is the most prevalent form of fighting in the Arab countries, which makes these people experts at hitting their targets. The girls cowered on the floor of the vehicle, urging Mel, who was driving, to "step on the gas, if we're going to make it back to the ship alive . . . !"

Mel did just that, nearly running some of the natives down on more than one occasion. "You have to remember how white European Christians have screwed up this part of the world to know why they're so pissed off," he yelled above the din.

"Maybe so," said Ginny, "but it's not fair to take it out on us, just because we happen to be the same color as their enemies."

"I agree," said Paul. "This is no way to cement international relations." By then, Paul had already gotten hit by rocks a few times, in the arm and the shoulder, and it was a real shock to be greeted like that by people to whom he had done no wrong, particularly since they weren't in the country on any kind of political or religious mission. To be attacked simply for being white was very frustrating. As a result, they were not only blameless, they were defenseless, scared shitless, and had no recourse but to keep moving fast, and ducking.

Their adventures in the city of Tangier were a little less hazardous. At first, anyway. Once they left the vehicle and wormed their way through those narrow, crowded alleyways, there really wasn't enough room for anyone to take aim with a rock. But they would soon learn there were a lot of other pitfalls to watch out for.

The large marketplace, or *medinah*, as it was called in Arabic, was a system of twisting, turning passageways crammed full of merchandise, donkeys, goats, peddlers, and foodstuffs. Wherever they looked, they saw something colorful or exotic, like fortune tellers, snake charmers, belly dancers, and the ever-haggling "businessmen." The Arab merchants who hawked their wares clearly did not believe in the "soft sell." Usually they stood in the doorway and pulled you inside their shops, smiling slimily all the while.

Mel persistently warned the girls not to go off shopping by themselves. "Because of the way you gals're dressed, you'd better stay close to us."

"Big deal, Tarzan," quipped Ginny. "What makes you think you'd scare off all these potential rapists?"

"The gun I'm carrying, if you must know," said Mel. As assistant purser, he had a permit to arm himself, and he had been smart enough to think of this before leaving the ship. It was the custom for all Muslim women to cover their faces with veils; and that day, both girls' shoulders were bare, as they had dressed for the weather, which was hot and sultry. It is also forbidden for Muslim women to define the shape of their figures by the clothing they wear.

"The 'sack' dress is a perennial favorite over here," Mel told them, "as long as no one can tell where your knockers end and your waistline begins."

"Now he tells us," said Tina, who wore the flimsiest of playsuits.

"This isn't the first time you gals were warned how to dress in this country," Mel gave back, "so be careful."

But they soon realized that just the sight of those two white half-naked females prancing so freely down their streets was taken as a direct insult.

"Infidels!" the locals shouted at them. "Whores!"

Then it began—a few of the locals took it for granted these were a couple of Caucasian hookers, out on the town. They suddenly moved in on the girls, jostling them, grabbing handfuls of tits, ass, and anything else that looked ripe to them, smiling snakily all the while as they chattered out filthy suggestions and endearments.

Moving fast, Mel got between the girls and their would-be molesters, took his gun out of its holster, raised it above his head and fired off a shot. Like magic, the offending Arabs retreated, and even began apologizing and salaaming all over the place. Surprisingly enough, a few of them spoke a little English.

"A thousand pardons, good sirs," said one of them. "We did not know that the naked ones were with escorts."

"What did he call us?" asked Ginny.

"He called you 'naked,' honey," said Paul. "And I guess from a Muslim's eye-view, that's just how you look."

Full of fire and ferocity now, with the gun still in hand, Mel said, "You Arab dogs, you have no right to treat our women like that. You don't catch us taking liberties with *your* women, do you?"

"Not bloody likely," Paul muttered under his breath. "Of course, it might help if we could see what we were getting under all that yardgoods."

"But this is so outrageous," said Tina. "We don't even *like* men that way . . ."

". . . Especially if they smell the way these do," Ginny added.

"Cool it," said Mel, ushering them away and out of danger. "This is no time to get them on the defensive again now that I've got them feeling so guilty."

After Mel's big "rescue," the girls apologized for causing so much trouble, promising never to make that same mistake again. To prove it, their first purchases in the market were a pair of all-covering caftans, complete with hoods. From then on, they were no longer hassled.

Nevertheless, during the rest of their stay in Tangier, they were always aware that sin and evil lurked at every corner. Not for nothing was Tangier known as the Crossroads of the World, for it was a fascinating mélange of mixed races and a surprisingly conglomerate city, with everything from robed Riffs to expatriate American artists attracted by the low prices and ever-mild climate. And yet, behind that glamorous façade — and particularly in the older sections of the city — the shipmates had the feeling they were surrounded by thieves, smugglers, pimps, and dope-pushers, not to mention fugitives-from-justice of every known nationality.

"The asshole of the world," Mel put it, as only someone raised on the streets of Brooklyn could sum it up.

"True," said Paul. "And yet, there's so much life here, so much daily struggle for survival. It seems to be an endless conflict for these people. I don't suppose they ever know what it means to feel tranquil or secure."

But on their last day in port, while the others chose to remain on the ship, Paul went shopping alone. Not being a half-naked woman, he was certain he'd have nothing to fear. But all too quickly it was brought home to him that not even a man as tall and well-built as he would be completely secure on his own. Certainly, he had done enough advance homework about this part of the world to know how anxious the Arabs were to lure white tourists away from the security of their group. Nonetheless, without realizing it, that was exactly what Paul allowed to happen that day while he went wandering through the stalls.

A smiling merchant approached him and said, "May I know what you are looking for?"

"I want to buy a nice leather hat," Paul told him, relieved that the man spoke English and he wouldn't have to rely on sign language.

"Ah yes, then follow me, please," the man said. "I know just the place."

And like an imbecile, Paul did just that. Simply because he was a man, he assumed the ground rules they had tried to enforce on the girls did not apply to him. So there he was, making the mistake of wandering far afield on his own. He followed the merchant down one twisted alleyway after the other until, before he knew it, he had completely lost his sense of direction and had no idea where he was.

Suddenly, he found himself in a shop surrounded by four smiling Arabs who were smoking hashish and making deals, trying to sell him everything in the shop. He found the leather hat he wanted, but the price was so outrageous, Paul smiled and kept saying, "No, I don't think so." Then they

137

smiled some more and got very sociable, insisting he would feel more relaxed if he smoked some of their hashish.

"Wouldn't happen to have a Lucky Strike on you, would you, gentlemen?" But that seemed to get them very angry and scowling. Not wanting to offend them further, he smoked a few puffs — and realized he was stoned out of his mind within a matter of seconds. Which surprised him, as the smoke had had such a mild taste. But one big whiff and he felt like Ali Baba chatting with the forty thieves. Indeed, he got so high so fast, he almost forgot to be afraid of the fact that he was about to be ambushed by a pack of snarling sodomists and he didn't know where the hell he was.

Good God, he thought, I've lost my bearings, which makes me one big vulnerable idiot, surrounded by the enemy and open to attack. "Listen, gentlemen," he chuckled, "it's been delightful, shooting the breeze with you, but now I have to get back to civilization. Oh . . . not that you fellows aren't civilized, of course . . . didn't mean that . . ."

He edged his way toward the exit, but his four grinning admirers kept moving in closer, and now he really felt tipsy from the combined effects of the hashish and their godawful breath which, though he couldn't identify it at the moment, had the faint aroma of camel-spit. He also felt an aura of sinister evil envelop him as they moved in closer and began grabbing at him, just about everywhere. Recalling how "convertible" these guys were when it came to sexual diversion, Paul now knew how the girls had felt when faced with the same danger. In short, his anal virginity was at stake and he was ready to fight for it.

One of the men offered him another toot on his pipe. "Big handsome American like to get high, is it not so?"

"No, it's not so," said Paul. "I'm not an American. No indeed, I'm a big handsome . . . uh, I mean, I'm British, and you wouldn't believe how ugly I can look when I put my mind to it." To demonstrate, he made a really grotesque face for them, even crossing his eyes. But they weren't buying. They kept pushing the hashish at him, and he said, "No thanks, I prefer to roll my own," smiling at them again now that the gross facial contortions hadn't worked. And still they kept pushing in closer and getting cozier, eyeing him up and down, then discussing him in Arabic, among themselves, as if he were a side of beef.

Christ! he thought. They're trying to figure out who gets the first piece of me. Now that he was convinced they had some dark and dirty designs on his derrière, he felt a surge of self-preservation take hold of him and he wrenched away from them, running toward the door. Two of the guys leapt forward, seizing him by the arms, one of them saying, "Ah, but you cannot leave us yet. We have so much more to show you."

"I've seen it," said Paul, then shoved them aside and started wildly sprinting out the door. Whatever they wanted from him, or with him, he wasn't having any. So he ran. Luckily, he'd always kept himself in pretty good shape by working out in the ship's gym, and was usually a fairly fast runner though, in the past, he always knew where he was going. So there he was, stoned in Tangier, running crazily through those alleyways, cutting back and forth, frantic, on an Asiatic "high," and terrified.

He looked back once and saw that two of his pursuers were still chasing him. He ran faster, feeling lost and disoriented and so damned uncertain. Running through those alleyways was like being lost in a maze. They were just wide enough for him to pass through, but so dark and narrow that he couldn't see the sun or the sky, so his sense of direction couldn't be relied upon.

Finally, he reached the opening of the marketplace and saw several people he remembered from the ship, even a few of his women customers and their husbands. When the guys who had been chasing him saw that he was once again among friends, they stopped in their tracks and retreated.

"Why, look, Hipatia," said one of his ladies to another, "there's Paul! That *is* him, isn't it, the one who styles our hair so beautifully?"

"Yes, of course, Eloise, that's him," said the one called Hipatia. "You think I could ever forget that wonderful face?"

"A pretty sweaty face, if you ask me," said her husband.

"Hello, Paul, dear," said Eloise. "Whatever have you been up to? And why do you look so winded?" Paul smiled at them. In that moment, he wanted to throw his arms about both those ladies, and would have, if their husbands hadn't been on the scene. "Actually, I've been jogging," he said. "You know, to keep fit and trim."

"Jogging?" asked one of the husbands. "In this awful heat?"

"Well, you know what they say about mad dogs and Englishmen," Paul gave back.

"Now there's a man who swears undying allegiance to his body," said Hipatia, looking at Paul as if she wanted to do the same. "You keep it up, dear, and who knows, you may be in perfect shape for the Olympics next year."

Later Paul kept thinking of what might have happened to him in that precarious situation if he hadn't taken some action when he did. How quickly those Arab sleazeballs could have knocked him unconscious or rendered him completely helpless with drugs and, after that happened, he didn't even want to think what might have befallen him — like total disappearance, for instance, without leaving a trace.

Although he usually enjoyed sharing his adventures with his friends on the ship, this time he had second thoughts about it. What should he tell them — that while hunting for bargains he almost got sold down the river in the process? Besides, he wasn't that eager to tell Ginny and Tina that he'd come even closer to losing his virtue than they had. And he could well imagine how fast this gossip would spread if he told his friend Mel about it. This was one colorful tale he kept to himself.

THIRTEEN

It was in late October of 1956, on what would turn out to be Paul's final voyage on the *Chusan* — and, indeed, his last year's hitch as a ship's hairdresser — that he broke the company's cardinal rule and fell madly in love with a fellow crew member.

As luck would have it, Joanna Carroll was not a "fellow," not by any stretch of the imagination. She was the first lady cruise director with whom Paul had ever come in contact. When they met aboard the *Chusan* during that long voyage to Africa and South America, Paul learned that this was not her first experience at sea, as she had served aboard other liners for the past year. Joanna was tall, attractive, and very poised. At twenty-six, she was a Canadian who had, at first, studied to be a nurse, then changed her mind and gone to college for two years. But finally, she changed her mind again when the urge to travel began to dominate all her ambitions. She worked at a travel agency in Toronto for another year or so, then became a landlocked tour guide until, finally, she found a way to set sail for some of those faraway places she'd been dreaming about.

Joanna was beautiful, though not aggressively so. Perhaps this was because she chose not to accentuate her physical attributes and, instead, concentrated primarily on her winning personality and the aura of cool self-assurance she was able to project. She had dark auburn hair, sparkling green eyes, a full, sensuous mouth, and a figure that was a lot more amply endowed than Paul realized when they first met. Indeed, it was because Joanna was so determined not to flaunt herself as a sex object that Paul was so certain that she wasn't his type, romantically speaking. As a result, he felt safe in cultivating her as a friend, assuming there would be no danger that a career-oriented, no-nonsense girl like Joanna would light his fire.

While it was true there was no instant flame ignited between these two, in time she had him flickering on all burners. But even that came as a total surprise for both of them.

Joanna had studied anthropology in college, and Paul later concluded it was because she was so much brighter than he that he'd assumed he would never respond to her sexually. She knew so much about the customs of the natives in every port they hit, he assumed that all he wanted from her was to pick her brain for hours on end. In reality, neither of them suspected how serious their involvement would become, even when they must have sensed their friendship was subtly changing into something else.

For one thing, everything was against it. At least while they were afloat. They both knew the rules, which forbade this kind of fraternizing among the employees. And over the years, Paul had been extra careful not to get too chummy with any of the female employees with whom he occasionally socialized. He made a point to see them only in groups, not on real dates. His friend Roy Tolliver, who was again working with him aboard the *Chusan,* was a perfect example of what could happen to a man when he let on-the-job temptation lead him astray. Roy and his little switchboard operator, Madge Barton, had conducted a hot and heavy affair, both on and off the ship. At the time, Roy had admitted to Paul that he'd never had any plans to marry her, that she was nothing more than a very enjoyable convenience for him. He assumed she was equally as lighthearted about their affair.

Then Madge got pregnant, but didn't tell Roy about it for months, fearing they would both lose their jobs. She actually waited until her condition was clearly obvious to anyone who glanced her way. When she was given her notice to leave the ship at the end of the current voyage, she insisted that the father had been a total stranger she'd taken up with while they were in port, in Sydney, Australia, refusing to involve Roy with her problem. Because of the long-term gossip about them, everyone knew that Roy was the father but, since they had been careful not to be caught "in the act," no one confronted Roy with any such accusations.

When the ship returned to Southampton at the end of that voyage, Madge went ashore. She later wrote Roy that she'd had her baby, a boy, and had given it up for adoption at once. Three months after that, Madge married a "nice, solid London businessman," and settled down. Roy always told Paul that that had been one of the most hazardous, narrow escapes of his entire seagoing career. "But it convinced me of something important," he added. "Now I know I want to stay free, single, and seagoing for as long as I'm able."

All that had happened four years earlier, and Roy seemed just as happy as ever to be doing exactly what he was doing, and having what he called "my bedtime frolics" only during visits ashore.

Nevertheless, Paul had kept Roy's example in mind as a constant reminder of what *not* to do with a female employee, no matter how enticing. It was generally felt that if the ship's employees got too intimate, it would detract from the performance of their duties. Gradually, Paul would begin to doubt the validity of this theory. Indeed, the more he saw of Joanna, the sillier and the more outdated that company rule began to seem. Until finally, Paul saw the example set by Roy Tolliver as something that could never happen the same way for him. Actually, what Roy and Madge had going was a rather shoddy little backstairs affair, having themselves a fast hump wherever they could swing it. Paul couldn't see himself embroiled in anything so demeaning. And certainly it wasn't anything he would want for himself and a superior girl like Joanna Carroll.

In the beginning, it was their work that kept them much too occupied to identify the spark that linked them whenever they were together. As cruise director, Joanna was obliged to pay attention to the needs of the passengers at all hours of the day and night and, in general, she was expected to try her level best to add to their feeling of comfort and ease. Those varied duties often turned her into a Jill-of-all-trades, running errands, serving in the capacity of social worker or nurse's aide, or often it would entail just being a companion to some of the elderly people who might be traveling alone.

Paul soon realized that aboard a luxury liner, the cruise director had to be all things to all people, which really meant she was required to socialize with just about everybody. This didn't bother him until he observed how effortlessly charming Joanna was with the rich, young male passengers, some of them married and some of them not.

During this voyage, Paul enjoyed a reunion with his good pal, Jason Rutledge, as he was still the *Chusan's* chief purser. When Paul told Jason he didn't think it was quite right that Joanna Carroll should have to ingratiate herself with so many leering and unattached male passengers, Jason gave his friend a suspicious look.

"What do you mean, not quite 'right'? Hell, that's her job. She's here to sell charm and TLC, and she does it very well. People seem to like having her around, and that's part of it, too."

"Sure, I know the job description of cruise directors. But I think that worked better when they were men. I mean, nobody thinks it's tacky when a guy walks up to a table where another guy is sitting alone and passes the time of day, just to cheer him up. But when a young woman does that, what's the first thing most people think?"

Jason gave him a crafty smile. "If that woman happens to be the ship's cruise director, they'll probably think she's a very conscientious worker."

"Yeah, well I think it's beneath her dignity."

"Hey, Paul, what's coming off here? You're not about to pull a Roy Tolliver on me, are you?"

Paul glared at him. "What the hell does that mean?"

"It means just what you think it means, that you've got the hots for that tall, queenly egghead."

"Don't be crazy," Paul said. "I was simply stating that, in my opinion, she's too nice and well-bred to have to come on like some kind of dancehall hostess. It's a different matter when the old ladies need her, or in case someone gets sick, or when she's arranging certain social activities for them to do on the ship . . ."

"Oh, I get it," said Jason. "But when she extends her favors to dancing with some unattached guy, that's when the old green-eyed monster, jealousy, gets your balls in an uproar, right?"

"No, smartass!" Paul said, a little surprised at his own vehemence. "You grind everything down to the basics, as if there's only one way for a man to relate to a woman: as a phallic conquest."

"Hell no," Jason chuckled, for he wasn't in the least offended. "I wouldn't say that's the only way, but it's sure a great start. On the other hand, young man, as chief purser on this ship, I strongly advise you two to reserve that sort of action for later, like when you're on dry land."

"What the hell kind of 'action' are you talking about? Believe me, Jason, it's not like that. We see each other now and then, for breakfast or lunch, and we talk. And those were conversations I thoroughly enjoyed. She's terribly bright, you know, and extremely well-read."

"Yeah, I know," said Jason. "That's what turned me off about her."

"Are you saying you actually made a pass at her?"

"Oh, I put out a few feelers, and man, she gave me such a frost, I half expected to turn to stone. Which is okay with me anyway, because I don't like my women to be brainier than I am."

"Oh really?" Paul said, grinning. "Well hey, that's good to know. The next time I meet a gorgeous pushover who hasn't got all her marbles, I'll tell her keeper to send her straight to you."

Actually, it wasn't until the first time Paul did Joanna's hair that it fully dawned on him that the chemistry between them was not platonic.

When a man does a woman's hair, he must touch that woman in certain places which, in normal circumstances, he would never think of as being erogenous. A woman's neck, her ears, cheeks, temples or, in Joanna's case, long flowing tresses of hair the color of burnt chestnut with glints of titian. In the past, such moves had all been terribly routine for Paul Barrington.

Initially, Joanna had sought out his services because, as she put it, "After all, you're the shop manager, so you must be the best."

This was a time when they had been acquainted for about ten days, during the first leg of the voyage as they cruised along Africa's Gold Coast. They had lunch together on occasion, and the sort of non-flirting conversations that had convinced them both there was no earthly reason for them not to be friends. Then came that very busy Saturday morning when she sat down in Paul's booth and he ran his fingers through her silken hair just once.

She eyed him in the mirror as he stood behind her and said, "You have beautiful hair," his fingers trailing lower, now toying with her ear lobes. "It has its own scent, you know, and will probably have the same scent, even after I've washed it, because it's yours, your very own personal perfume . . ."

He was babbling and he couldn't stop. It was as if he were in a trance, or, perhaps, hypnotized by the look she was giving him in the mirror, a look that had grown very intense. Her skin felt hot to the touch, and soft.

"Can you draw that curtain around us?" she asked.

He nodded, not removing his hands from their contact with her flesh. "You want privacy?" he asked, almost whispering.

"I think it's best," she said. "Don't you?"

It had, of course, "happened" for them both in the same moment. So he drew the curtain, then turned on one of the faucets in the sink to mask the sound of their voices.

"It *is* safe in here, isn't it?" she asked, then let out an involuntary giggle.

"Safe, yes," he said, "but not very roomy."

She reached for his hands and lowered them, until they struck an impasse Paul hadn't counted on — her breasts were so much fuller and more voluptuous than he'd imagined. Jesus! he thought, as she pressed his hands against them, what the hell am I doing?

"We're being very crazy, Paul," she said, as if reading his mind. "But I really think we've *got* to start meeting like this, because you and I both know that if we do this anywhere else on the ship, we'll lose our jobs."

Now his heart was racing so fast, he could hardly breathe.

"Do *what,* Joanna? Tell me . . ."

"I want you to kiss me," she said. "I think I must have been wanting that for weeks."

149

He whirled around in front of her, then swept down and took her in his arms, bib and all. Gently, he began to kiss her, lightly dabbing his lips against hers, tracing and swirling tenderly over the warm and fragrant breath-scent, then wrapping his arms completely about her and deepening the kiss, groaning as he crushed his open mouth more fully and succulently against hers, going braver and hungrier for everything about this girl he suddenly wanted to devour. He held her closer and felt the hot round thrust of her breasts shoving against him, moving his hands lower, then higher . . . and she felt so explosively alive in his arms. But then he realized he was in such an excited state of arousal, he didn't dare go any farther. Not here and now.

"Oh, God, darling, careful!" He lurched backwards so abruptly, he squatted down hard in a sinkful of scalding water, thoroughly soaking, and burning the seat of his pants.

He let out a gasp and, as he met her eyes, they both started to giggle at the same time, muffling the sounds with their hands. "Hot pants. . !" he muttered.

"No, don't!" she whispered. "Did you have to say it?"

Now that the heat of the moment was somewhat dampened, they looked at each other again, in all seriousness.

"Oh God," he said, "what're we going to do? I want you so much, and now that I know you feel the same way, I want to let out a roar and shout it from the rooftops. But Jesus, not like this. I mean, this is nuts, in here like a couple of nasty little kids. Come to my cabin tonight, Joanna. Or would it be better if I came to yours?"

"No," she said firmly. "Neither of us can afford to take a chance like that. I think we should be grateful we have this."

"This?" he said, gaping around their little stall. "In here, with all that activity going on around us? You want to drive me crazy?"

150

"But you're the manager, Paul, so no one would dare undrape that curtain while you're busy with a customer, isn't that right?"

"Yes, I suppose so, but how would I account for all the time we spend in here? I mean . . . if we make love in here, which just may be impossible, and you emerge with your hair untouched . . . "

"But of course you'll do my hair," she said. "Do you think I'd let you become a malingerer, with a reputation like yours to uphold? Besides, it will keep people from getting suspicious."

The harder Paul tried to make some sense of this, the more absurd it seemed. "Look, sweetie, I . . . I really don't know if I can do both at the same time."

"Come on, Paul," she said, giving him a defiant smile, "don't tell me this is the first chance you've had to be ambidextrous on the job."

"No, it's not," he said. "But it's the first time I ever planned to do anything about it."

"Well, obviously we can't do everything," she said, "the logistics being what they are. Which means you needn't worry about despoiling my virginity even if I still had it, which I don't, I assure you. But at least we can become sort of semi-engaged in here. You know, what we used to call 'heavy necking' when I was in high school."

He gaped at her. "Good God, you mean that's *all?*"

"While we're on board this ship, it is. And you know as well as I that it had better be. Somehow we must manage to do absolutely everything together except have intercourse. Then nobody can accuse us of having an affair — at least, not technically."

"But gosh, that sounds so . . . so nervewracking," he said. "What do I mean, 'nervewracking'? It sounds like torture . . ."

151

"Still, it's all we have at the moment, Paul, so stop wasting precious time and kiss me again. I love the way you do it, Paul, as if you could die for my kisses, and your mouth is so full and hot . . ."

Hearing this, he let out a helpless little groan, thinking if it turned out this girl was merely a tease or some weird kind of game-player, he couldn't really care at the moment, even though he had a feeling he would learn to hate this test of his endurance very quickly. Then they eyed each other in silence for a moment, and they knew they had to take whatever they could get for now. Paul knew that for him, their first kiss had already seemed like a lifetime investment, so he had to believe they would eventually draw on it together.

"Okay," he said, "but I think we should switch positions."

"Oh?"

"Let me sit in the chair. Then I'll cuddle you in my lap, okay?"

"I love it!" She quickly undid her blouse, unsnapped her bra, so that by the time she nestled in his lap, her marvelous breasts were all loose and dangling and so happily accessible, Paul immediately went a little drunk with flesh.

They necked feverishly for about five minutes, then Paul got a little crick in his neck as he leaned lower and lower, yearning to gobble up as much of her as he could manage. "Oh, God, I want all of you, Joanna . . . want the rest of you and the best of you . . . !"

"Oops!," she said, glancing at her watch, "time's up. You'd better stop all that kissing and do my hair now. And quickly. Make it something simple, but stylish, of course."

Moving like a man in a semi-catatonic stupor, Paul rose, muttering, "Of course, Milady." He moved around behind her, then let out a gasp as he pressed his lingering rigidity a bit too fiercely against the back of the chair.

"What's the matter, Paul? You didn't break it, did you?"

"The chair?"

"No, silly, your thingamabob."

"Almost, but it's on the bend . . . I mean, on the mend. Oh hell, this is going to kill me!"

"Now tell me, dear, do you think I should have an egg shampoo first, and then something in a bouffant upsweep?"

He glared furiously at her in the mirror. "A fine romance this is going to be."

"Why, whatever do you mean?"

"All foreplay and no volcanoes."

She laughed softly. "Yes, but think how much more we'll appreciate those volcanic disturbances when they finally erupt all over us, on shore."

That was their beginning. And since it would be another three weeks before they arrived at the next port, Paul was about to find out what it felt like to live in danger.

FOURTEEN

Never had Paul Barrington faced a more maddening ordeal than those next three weeks on board the *Chusan*. It would be a long and leisurely voyage before they were due to dock in Rio de Janeiro. At that time, he and Joanna would have a full five days ashore together to assuage their frustrations, though Paul seriously doubted he would last that long.

During those first ten days, Joanna had her hair done every other day, and true to her word, that was the extent of their time alone together. To make matters worse, the ship was loaded with passengers, most of them women who demanded Paul's services even more often than usual. Consequently, the state of his nerves and hormones during the rest of that voyage kept him lovestruck whenever he was able to hold Joanna in his arms for their turbulent kisses and fingerdancing, and frozen in heat whenever they were apart.

Paul grew more certain they could have arranged something more "comfortable," if they put their minds to it, but he suspected Joanna was enjoying the intrigue of playing with fire each time they drew the curtain around Paul's booth and started grabbing handfuls of each other between kisses. He couldn't believe he was permitting any woman to toy with him in this manner, letting her call all the shots according to her own dictates, while she blandly shoved all his wishes aside. When he realized he was genuinely in love with her, it began to worry him that she was only using him for recreation, not romance. More than once he had told her, "Darling, I think I'm in love with you."

"But of course you are," she would reply. "Do you think I'd let you take all these liberties with me if you were not?"

Which still sounded suspiciously like a one-sided deal to him, for it only meant that she fully believed in his sincerity but wasn't about to make any such commitments of her own. As a result, he began to suffer long, restless nights of insomnia, and now whenever he observed Joanna socializing with some of the male passengers, he grew more paranoid and suspicious about her than ever.

Ironically enough, Paul was certain that he and Joanna weren't really fooling that many people during those next weeks. Roy Tolliver, for one, knew exactly how and where Paul was, as he put it, "getting your licks in," almost from the start.

He actually congratulated Paul on his ingenuity. "Now I'm convinced what a really creative artist you are, Paul," Roy told him. "Imagine, having the guts to work in a little jazzy sport-fucking while you're doing some bird's hair. Frankly, I would never have had the courage to try that, even with Madge. Of course, we used to do it under stair-wells, in linen closets, and once or twice, late at night, under the canvas in a lifeboat. But right here in the shop? I think it's gorgeous, the way you're able to get away with it."

Luckily, Paul was too busy to reply when Roy first paid him these tributes. But he finally told him it wasn't what he thought, that he and Joanna did not, as yet, have carnal knowledge of each other, only "semi-carnal."

"Sure, I know," Roy grinned devilishly. "But don't you worry, old pal, your dirty secret is safe with me."

"But dammit, Roy, it's not as frivolous as it seems. I'm serious about this girl, and that's never happened to me before. In fact, I have a feeling we're going to have a long and beautiful future together."

"Are you mad? A hard-bitten career girl like her? Don't count on it. It's clear she's only using you for a little ship-board stud-service."

"That's a shitty thing to say!" Paul said in a fury. "It's not true. Certainly if she wanted that sort of thing, she has plenty of opportunities with some of the rich and eligible young male passengers she meets."

"Ah, but she can't have her way with them as safely as she can with you, Paul, hidden from view in the draped booth of a beauty parlor."

"Dear God, you call that 'safe'?" Paul demanded. "Why, these have been the most frantic experiences I've ever had in my life. What's more, I'm quite sure my blood pressure goes up every time it happens. And no matter what you think, we haven't gone all the way yet, because it's really quite impossible in that cramped situation, and I'm sure by the time we are able to have each other that way, I'll have had a stroke from hypertension, not to mention the threat of accidental ejaculation at a time when I'm due to wait on the next customer the minute Joanna is through with me. Believe me, Roy, it's bloody hell, and stop all that laughing . . . !"

"Oh, Paul, no matter what you say, you two *are* safe behind that curtain. It's only an old pro like me who might know the score. The point is, nobody in the world would suspect what you're doing, right in the middle of the shop. That's why it's working. Of course, if you want to give it a rest, I'll be glad to fill in for you next time around."

When they still had another ten days at sea before they were due to dock in Rio, Joanna told Paul that the gossip among their shipmates was beginning to spread, and it was worrying her.

They still had their "platonic" lunches and breakfasts together, at which times they tried very hard not to give each other longing looks; and, of course, there was no touching. Nevertheless, Joanna said one of the nurses had made a few remarks. "She said she didn't blame me in the least for finding you attractive, as she thinks you're quite a dreamboat."

"Some dreamboat," he said. "I feel as if I've been scuttled every time you walk off and leave me throbbing and unfulfilled in my little stall."

"Nevertheless, I'll have to think of something to offset these rumors," said Joanna. "Of course, like an idiot, I told her you were an old friend of the family, and she said that had to be a far-flung family, with me raised in Canada and you in London. Then I told her you were a long-lost cousin, twice removed, and that it was in our family's blood to do a great deal of traveling."

"And what did she say to that?"

"Oh, she just smiled and walked away, the bitch! Of course, there's no way she could know for sure, since neither of us has ever been seen heading for the other's cabin late at night."

"Right now, I wish we *had* been seen like that," he said. "Think of the luxury and the expanse, of having you in a bed. God, right now I'm so hungry for that, I'd even be willing to keep the door open while we did it."

"Don't be such a child!"

"No, I mean it, Joanna. I'm at the point where I've about *had* the life of a . . . a fingerwaving sailor, so for me I really think it's worth the sacrifice if they find out about us and fire me. It's time I started thinking of a more solid future for myself, perhaps back in London, at least for a start. What I really want is my own shop someday, you know. That's what I've been saving for . . . "

"Well, yes, I can understand that," she said, "but certainly you'd want a good reference, not some shoddy scandal hanging over your head. After all the years you've spent at sea, why should you give them the chance to fire you, simply for falling in love?"

158

It was such a heady novelty for her to be using those words, Paul said nothing for a moment; he simply smiled at her. "Say that again," he said.

"What do you mean?"

"Say 'falling in love' again, only this time switch it around so that it sounds as if you're doing as much of the falling as I am."

She smiled. "Now, Paul, surely you must know how I feel about you by this time, after where I've been putting my hands on you."

He nodded, newly aroused by the little word-picture she'd just painted. "But I want more."

"Well, that will come. Now please stop looking at me like that. I've got to rush. Meanwhile, I'll be thinking of a way to throw everybody off the scent."

The next evening, Paul and Jason were in the ship's main cocktail lounge together, seated at the bar, when Paul glanced in the mirror over the bar and saw the reflection of something very unsettling. It was Joanna, looking radiant and sumptuously gowned as she entered the room on the arm of a very affluent-looking guy who appeared to be old enough to be her father. Paul kept staring as they sat down at a table for two.

Jason saw them come in at the same time. "Hey, look at that, Paul. Our Joanna is really hitting the big time."

Paul clenched his fists for a moment, trying not to reveal what he was feeling. He downed half his highball in one sloshing gulp, then went into a little coughing fit. Jason slapped him on the back, then ordered him a straight shot of Scotch.

"Cool it, Paul," he said. "She's just doing her job. I'm sure that old fart couldn't begin to compete with what she gets from you, even if he is something of a billionaire."

Paul turned and glared at him. "Oh Jesus, does everybody on the ship know about us?"

159

"Don't worry. Roy made me promise not to tell anyone else. Frankly, I'm all for it, and if you can actually build up any leverage behind that booth, more power to you. Me, I'd need an awful lot more room to spread her out in."

"Who *is* that sonofabitch?" Paul growled. "It's bad enough he looks rich, he also looks familiar."

"He should," said Jason. "He's always getting a lot of international press. That's Andrew Steadwell, a super-loaded automobile tycoon from Detroit, four times married and as rich as Croesus."

"He looks ancient."

"Oh, I guess he's about fifty-three or thereabouts," said Jason. "And from what I've heard, he's led the life of a typically jaded American sultan. You know, a real cocksman with a diamond-studded mistress and/or concubine in every port."

"Thanks a lot, pal. That's really a lot more than I wanted to know about him."

About ten minutes later, after a quick drink, the happy, laughing couple left the bar, arm in arm. Paul kept telling himself this was her plan to offset the gossip about them. And yet, what about the sort of gossip that might very well spread about her and one of the passengers? Wasn't that equally as *verboten?* And surely, he thought, that would be a lot more noticeable than their so-brief and hidden little pattycake assignations.

Later that night, he wandered casually into the ballroom and saw them dancing together. Look at the risk she's taking, he thought, to stay with the same passenger all night. When she happened to notice him over Steadwell's shoulder, she gave him a friendly smile and waved. Paul was infuriated to think she might be trying to make him jealous when she *knew* he wasn't permitted to do anything about it. Yet he had to stand by and watch them laughing it up and exchanging a lot of lewd eye-signals with each other. Certainly she had to be revolted by the thought of a dilapidated old roué like that panting for her body.

Unable to watch them any longer, he went to his cabin for some serious brooding and thinking. By midnight, he was still unable to relax, much less sleep. Deciding to break another of her commandments, he telephoned her cabin.

"Joanna? Sorry to call at this hour. Did I wake you?"

"Oh, Paul, it's you," she said, her voice languid and rather husky, which gave him the idea she might not be alone. "What's up?"

"Look, I know you want to throw everybody off the scent about us, but aren't you going from the frying pan into the fire?"

She sighed. "Oh, dear. I suppose you're talking about Andrew."

"Oh, so it's on a first-name basis already, is it? Dammit, Joanna, you'd better be careful being seen with someone that well-known, or somebody might send a report about you to the company."

"Oh, really? Who, for instance?"

"Me, for instance! You could end up breaking a lot more rules with him than you've ever done with me . . . *and* getting your picture on the front page, to boot . . . !"

That really broke her up. She laughed for a full thirty seconds, which had Paul wondering if Steadwell were laughing right along with her, in bed, maybe, and if so, how could she bear to let that old lecher touch her when all *he'd* been able to do was have her in his lap? Damn the bitch, it wasn't fair!

"Dear Paul," she said, "don't you realize it's because this man is so well-known that I'm using him to divert all attention from us? And with him I have the built-in excuse to socialize with him, as part of my duties as cruise director. While with you, there's practically no excuse at all, except to get my hair done." She started laughing again. "And darling, I must tell you that there's a limit to how long we can keep *that* up before I start going bald . . . !"

Paul was not amused. And besides, he felt that anyone who would use the word "bald" in the presence of a hairdresser had to be crass and insensitive.

"Okay, Joanna, let's get serious here," he said. "Answer me this: just how far do you plan to go with this human decoy?"

"A harmless flirtation, Paul, and that's all I want."

"Have you broken this news to Steadwell?"

"You needn't worry about him. He already knows I've no intention of having some grungy little affair with him. He has made his subtle suggestions and he's been rebuked. And since he's a man of the world, and much hungrier for companionship than he is for sex — he's *had* all that anyway, to hear him tell it — he's not going to press the matter. He will simply be satisfied with my company and conversation."

"But he's so old," said Paul. "What could you two possibly find to talk about?" Then the thought hit him. "His money? Oh, Joanna, if that's true I know I'll never be able to compete with him. The way I hear it, this guy can afford to buy and sell General Motors, so naturally he'd be able to fit you into his budget without lifting a finger."

"Oh, Paul, do you really think I'm that mercenary?"

"I don't know. I guess that's what I'm trying to find out."

"Well, it's true that Andrew is filthy-rich, right?"

"They don't come much filthier."

"Okay, then you have nothing to worry about," she said. "My parents are very nicely fixed, which means I was *not* traumatized by an impoverished childhood. They head up their own real estate dynasty, if you must know, and back home there are certain funds being held in trust for me which guarantee that I will never have to marry for anything but love. Now, does that satisfy your curiosity for the night?"

"Yes, I suppose so," he said, though he secretly felt it only proved she'd had a lot of comfort in her life, not the kind of fairy-tale luxury an Andrew Steadwell could provide.

"Paul, listen to me," she said, "it's important to me that you believe what I've said about Andrew. All I want is to get us safely through to Rio, and with both our careers still intact, because I have news for you: no matter how much financial security I may have, I plan to be a working wife if we get married. No vegetation or dry rot for me. Are you ready for that?"

"Wait a minute," he said, "I'm still trying to get ready for that part about us 'getting married.' So far, neither of us has even mentioned marriage before, and suddenly here you are, my working wife . . . !"

"Well, I thought it was time one of us mentioned what's been on our minds all these weeks," she said.

"But . . . not working on a ship, though," he said, thinking aloud. "I mean, if I have a shop in London, you can't be shipping out, unless I change my plans and I . . . "

". . . Or," she broke in, "I could start my own little travel agency."

"Yes, yes," he said, growing more excited. "Oh, God, Joanna, you're not just saying all this to get me to hang up, are you?"

"No," she laughed, "but it's a thought. I'm getting very sleepy, aren't you?"

"I love you, Joanna," he said. "And I trust you, too. I mean it. From now on, I won't even let out a quiver of jealousy when I see you and Steadwell together. You go on doing whatever you have to, and I'll go on believing the truth, that you're doing it all for us, okay?"

"Sounds fine, darling. And now shall we say goodnight?"

"Right. But first I've got one more little question."

"Okay," she said.

"Is he there with you now?"

163

Pause. And then, her *"What?!"*

"Steadwell, I mean. Is he there?"

She hung up.

Paul stared at the phone, unable to believe the incredible echo of his own words. How could I have been so verbally crude, he wondered, when mentally I was feeling so charming and sophisticated? What had happened to the message his brain was supposed to be sending to his mouth?

He called her back, to apologize. It rang eleven times and she didn't answer, so he hung up. And tried again in thirty seconds. This time it rang twice and she answered.

"Any more insults?" She sounded furious.

"No, baby . . . and I'm so sorry. I swear, I don't know what got into me."

"Very well, then, would you like to explain that to Andrew? He's right here, just a moment. Slide over to the phone, darling, it's Paul, that horny little hairstylist I was telling you about. He seems badly in need of reassurance . . . "

Paul's mouth fell open and his blood went cold, but suddenly he heard Joanna laughing like a wild thing.

"Oh, Paul, I'm sorry, but you deserve to be tortured after that last insinuation. And if I weren't so flattered and touched and just plain in love with the way you get jealous, I'd probably feel terribly offended, except that I don't because you're sweet and crazy and sexy, and now can we please call it a night?"

"I'll be right there."

"That is not what I was getting at, Paul, and you know it."

"Okay, then listen, Joanna, I really do love you and I trust you and believe you, too, and frankly, I never even knew I had a jealous streak in me until I met you."

"Is that all?"

"As long as you love me," he said. "Do you?"

"Don't you know that by now?" she said, and again hung up the phone.

"Of course I know it," he said aloud, the phone in his lap. And I trust her, too.

Just before he got into bed that night, Paul had a shot of Scotch to celebrate his complete undying faith in this woman. No more suspicion or jealousy or paranoid fears that a man as powerful and suave as Steadwell would have her all melted down and in his pocket by the time they got to Rio. No indeed; in Joanna he would meet his match, for she would be far too strong for him. Paul could just hear her coolly rejecting the guy when he offered to give her a ten million dollar bonus as a wedding prize: "No, Mr. Steadwell, a thousand times no. You cannot buy me, for I love only Paul. He may be poor. In fact, he barely has a pot to piss in, but he's mine . . . !"

God, how beautiful that sounded. Paul fell asleep, listening to that lovely refrain — "He's mine, he's mine . . ."

But he woke up at three a.m., in a cold sweat, wondering what right he had to demand utter fidelity from a woman like Joanna? With her beauty, brains, and personality, she could have kings and princes and potentates, so imagine the shame of her having to confess, "I married my hairdresser," which naturally implied she was so desperate, who else would have her? How could he ever hold someone like that? It would be like trying to ensnare a bolt of quicksilver. And even now, did he imagine he had any real claims on her?

No.

So far, there'd been nothing between them but a lot of greasy kid stuff, an agonizing carousel of kisses and tit-clutching, which was no way for a grown man and woman to behave, if they were committed to one another. So Paul decided maybe he'd be safer if he didn't believe in her quite so devoutly. That way, it wouldn't be nearly so devastating if, when they got to Rio, Joanna decided to walk off into the sunset with Steadwell instead of him. Certainly, if he allowed enough leeway in his mind to *expect* her to betray him, then nobody could get hurt.

Now that his problem was solved, he slept on it. Fitfully.

But the moment he awoke the next morning, another thought hit him: Damn! Why didn't I think to phone Steadwell's cabin last night to find out if he was where *he* belonged?

Oh no, he thought, oh ye of little faith, what am I saying? That, I could never stoop to. Because, as God is my witness, I trust this woman, I really do . . . to the ends of the earth. Maybe farther . . .

FIFTEEN

During the final week of their voyage to Rio, Joanna decided to cancel any further appointments to get her hair done until they were in port. She slipped Paul a little note, which read: "We'll have to be more careful from now on, darling, as people are beginning to talk about my frequent visits to your shop. Women, mostly, the green-eyed monsters. So let's keep up our cool façade until we're ashore. Meanwhile, Andrew continues to be our best job insurance at the moment."

This meant Paul would have to give up any kind of intimate contact with her. Earlier, he had felt nothing could be worse than seeing so little of her, and now, he was to have even less. Indeed, she was cutting off his supply without warning. Now he knew how drug addicts felt when they had to go "cold turkey." In the meantime, while he had none of her, he had to sit calmly by and watch Steadwell escort her for nightly cocktails, dinner and dancing. On occasion, they would join other high-echelon friends of Steadwell's, either married bluebloods or over-the-hill swingers like himself. It almost seemed as if Joanna were being adopted by a swarm of dilettantes, and it was in a most rarefied atmosphere she now very willingly found herself.

As he watched this charade from the sidelines, all of Paul's doubts and insecurities came back to haunt him. How could he believe she was only doing all this for appearances' sake when she made it clear how much fun she was having? The more he watched Steadwell in action, the more he detested the man. He could imagine what a big man on campus he must have been thirty years ago. Didn't he know what a sorry sight he was, trying to make out with a girl like Joanna who, Paul was beginning to think, deserved every creak in Steadwell's joints that was coming to her.

When Paul confided in Roy, his advice was a bit too realistic and cynical for him. "When you stop mooning around like some incurable lovestruck loon, you'll see the handwriting on the wall fast enough. And when that happens, you'll learn to be philosophical about it, the way I am. Believe me, it'll keep you from being hurt."

"By 'philosophical' I take it you mean I should forget all about Joanna and find someone new, right?"

"Do you really think there's an alternative? Certainly, you don't still buy her story about using Steadwell as job insurance, do you?"

"It does seem stupid, doesn't it? And yet, somehow I can't believe she could ever be serious about a man his age."

"If by 'serious' you mean you don't think she's madly in love with the guy, you're probably right. But in a transaction of this magnitude, there are a lot of other considerations that enter into it. Joanna's a girl who's thinking about her future. I can tell that by the way she looks at him."

"No, Roy, you don't know her or you couldn't say that. She's much too self-sufficient to become some rich man's plaything. What's more, she loves her job, loves to travel. . ."

"Of course, she loves to travel. Don't you know why most girls want jobs like these? Sure, to travel and see the world, but also to find themselves a rich husband."

"Oh, hell," Paul said with a despairing sigh. "If that's true, maybe I *should* take your advice and start getting a little philosophical. Maybe for me and Joanna, it was always inevitable. We were like two ships passing in the night, and now that we've lost sight of each other, it's all over."

"Now you're making some sense," said Roy. "And listen, tonight there's this very secretive party which nobody's supposed to know about. Only I know about it, and I think it would be just what the doctor ordered to boost your morale."

"What party?"

"Ray and Hal are throwing it, down in the baggage room which, as you know, is a really smashing place to have a party."

Ray and Hal were two young baggage clerks, a couple of fun-loving, amiable fellows who were the first male homosexuals Paul had ever encountered on the job. They were so "normal" looking, however, he had known them for months before Roy finally put him wise. Not only were they "queer," as Roy put it, they were devotedly queer for each other — lovers, in other words. After the novelty wore off, Paul found them very easy to talk to, as well as extremely witty and entertaining. As time passed, it actually began to slip his mind that these two guys were different from anyone else.

As for Jason Rutledge, he had his own reason for being so tolerant of these "odd ducks." In fact, he was all for hiring more men just like them. "Don't you see, the more of their kind on board ship, the less competition for the rest of us."

That night it was Hal's birthday, so they were planning a really outrageous jamboree in the baggage room, though it was against every known regulation to convert those premises as elaborately as they did. The whole room was festooned with banners and lanterns, and, as the *pièce de résistance*, both Hal and Ray planned to attend in drag.

"And I know a couple of girls on board who just might be able to upset their apple cart," Roy told Paul that morning. "These are two real cute sisters. One is twenty and the other is twenty-two."

"Oh? What part of the ship do they work in?"

"No, no, they're passengers, not employees."

Paul stared at him. "You mean, you're taking the risk of playing around with passengers, after all the lectures you gave me about Joanna?"

"Well, that was getting to be a heavy affair, Paul, but this is strictly playtime. Lord, I've actually been alternating, one sister one night, the other one the next."

"Where, for God's sake?"

"Oh, here and about. We manage to find the right places. What's more, I don't have to do their hair while I'm banging them."

"Neither did I, unfortunately," Paul said gloomily. "Joanna and I never did make it to ground zero, you know."

"Yes, and that's what's so sad about it," said Roy. "Anyway, when this started out it was only supposed to be with Felicia, the younger sister. It seems the older girl, Laura, is due to be married when she returns to the States, so this is to be her one last fling before she ties the knot. Felicia says this is her wedding present to her sister. So, after I had a roll in the hay with Felicia, she told her big sister about my staying power. So the next night I proved that I knew just what to get the girl who's about to take herself out of circulation forever. And get this: the other night I ended up in their cabin with both of them, and that was the best double-scoop ice cream cone I've ever had. Afterwards, the little bride-to-be kissed me and said, "Thank you, Roy. If it weren't for you, I might never have had what I'll probably be missing for the rest of my life."

"Jesus, that doesn't say much for the boy back home," said Paul.

"Yeah, that's what *I* thought. So, I said, 'Come on, little one, don't sell your fiancé short.' And then I asked her what kind of work he did. And you'll never guess what she said."

"Millionaire industrialist?" Paul said, his mind still on Andrew Steadwell.

"No, she just sighed very pensively and said, 'He's in Mortuary Science.'"

"Oh, no," said Paul. "Gee, that poor kid."

170

"That's what I wanted you to say, Paul, because she will be your date tonight. I figure you can both cheer each other up. What's more, you still have a few more days of the voyage to let Joanna see you with this new gal, know what I mean?"

"Yeah, I think I do," Paul said, starting to get excited about the evening for the first time. "Sure, if she can play around with a passenger for the sake of appearances, why can't I?"

"That's the spirit," said Roy. "Although tonight the girls won't look like any competition for Joanna."

"Why not?"

"Because we're going to play a cute little trick on Ray and Hal by having the girls go in drag. First of all, they won't be expecting any passengers down there, since everybody knows passengers aren't allowed below deck. So here's the plan: we make the boys think these two 'strangers' are two new guys working on the ship whom they haven't met as yet. Then the girls'll pretend to come on to both boys. As men, mind you, not women. And just when the four of them expect to make a night of it, the girls will unmask themselves and let the cat out of the bag. I've already been working on their costumes and makeup, and I'm sure Hal and Ray won't get offended. Those guys love a good joke, even when it's on them."

"Wait a minute, Roy," said Paul, his head spinning from this description. "Is all this going to be as confusing as it sounds?"

"What's confusing? The girls will go in costume, as men. And Since Ray and Hal will be in drag, as women, they'll be under the impression these two new guys have a big thing about transvestites and just can't wait to get under their skirts. Which gives us a classic case of boy meets girl, only in reverse."

"Well, I have to hand it to you, Roy," Paul said, laughing. "That's the most deliciously sick stunt you've ever come up with. Only one thing bothers me: where does that leave us at the end of the evening, if the two men who aren't men end up in bed with the two women who aren't women?"

Roy stared blankly at him for a few seconds. "Jesus, when you put it like that, it's enough to give you a headache. But you see, it won't ever get that far. The girls'll confess their masquerade in time, and then we get to cart them off."

"Dressed in men's clothes."

"Oh well, we'll soon get them out of those."

Actually, the evening didn't turn out exactly as expected. The most fun Paul had was helping Roy with the girls' costumes and makeup. As a project and a challenge, it was a welcome diversion for Paul, as it kept him from brooding over Joanna. They spent a lot of time and care to make these two beauties look like very young and comely men. They waxed their hair and pomaded it back in sleek pompadours, then used more wax to give the cosmetic illusion they each had beards or, at least, five o'clock shadows.

Roy particularly enjoyed helping the giggling "boys" camouflage their bouncy breasts, though he found it impossible to handle these maneuvers without getting emotionally involved. Finally, their creations looked perfect, so they started working on their voices, getting them to speak only in their lowest registers.

Paul found it a lot of antic fun, and also an excellent way to get acquainted with each of the girls. They were both pretty enough, and it was clear the one called Laura was more than pleased with Paul. He decided he would gladly take what she was offering, if only to end the aggravating, and rather sophomoric, sexual frustration he had known ever since Joanna first started teasing him with nothing but samples of things to come.

Later, neither Paul nor Roy would ever quite figure out how they managed to end up on the wrong side of the merry-go-round that night. Of course, there was a great deal of heavy drinking going on, and Paul did remember it was unexpectedly hot down there in the baggage room. So hot, in fact, that the wax they had used on the girls' hair and beards started to melt right down into their trousers. As a result, they looked and felt so "icky," as they put it, that they were forced to give away their surprise much earlier than planned. Then there were so many people, and so much going on, Paul lost track of time for awhile. The next thing he knew, the sisters were returning to the party, all freshly showered and changed into dresses. And they were not alone. With them were two of the ship's most handsome young officers.

"Where the hell did they come from?" Paul asked Roy.

"Oh, something borrowed along the way, most likely," said Roy. "But don't worry, Paul, as officers they'd never dare get involved with passengers, not with Captain Halprin running the ship."

After about another hour or so of games, music, and mad cavorting, Paul glanced at the exit just in time to see his date for the night slip away with one of the officers. Since her sister was nowhere to be found, he figured she must have gone off with her own captive in uniform long ago. Hell, he thought, I should have come in costume tonight, too: as a ship's officer. At the time, though, Paul was so pissy-eyed plastered, he couldn't really care who went where. Then, as the guests dwindled off, the true irony of their situation finally hit them—both girls were gone, while Paul and Roy were left with "the boys," who were still in drag.

Upon realizing this humiliating predicament, Paul gazed blearily at Roy and said, "What's wrong with this picture?"

Roy, who was even drunker, waved a finger at him and said, "You're absolutely right. The girls have cut out and we're left holding the bags."

Ray and Hal both laughed good-naturedly at this. "Incidentally, Roy," said Hal, "what happened to your big surprise tonight?"

Roy hiccoughed. Then he said, "It melted."

"Is that a fact?" Ray said, now doing an uncanny imitation of Mae West. "Well, then, to the victors belong the spoils. How about it, boys? Think you'd like to bunk in with us tonight and change your luck?"

"Thanks a lot," said Roy.

". . . But no thanks," added Paul.

"Actually," said Roy, "I make it a rule never to come between a man and his husband."

"Husband?" Ray howled. "In these clothes?"

"Whatever," said Roy. Then he looked at Paul. "Paul, you get the feeling the party's over?"

With that, Paul got up and stood at attention. "It's three o'clock in the morning. Do you people know where your cruise director is this very moment?"

"No," said Roy, crouching down for a leering Groucho Marx imitation, "and neither do you."

"Wrong, I know: she's in bedwell's stead. Oh, shit, that's not right . . . she's in the well with old Andrew and she just found out he'll never be able to get it up . . ."

". . . So she drowned him," Roy said. "End of movie and *finis*, and we'd better haul ass out of here before these two ladies start to look good to us."

By now, both Ray and Hal were laughing so hard, their wigs fell off, followed by their eyelashes. And by then, they were both too gassed, frazzled, and spent to do anything but pass out very conveniently while still in drag.

The party had, indeed, come to a crashing halt.

Paul and Joanna only managed to get together once more before the ship docked in Rio. Their "date" was for what Joanna called "a quickie breakfast, just so we can touch base." But after only a few minutes of being that close to her again, Paul knew he wanted to touch a lot more of her than that. His plan to treat her coldly and talk about his other current conquests fell by the wayside very quickly. Where she was concerned, he didn't care what happened to his dignity; he had to believe they had a future together.

"Everything's been so damned social, Paul, I haven't had a moment to myself."

"I've noticed," he said miserably.

"But you've been in my thoughts constantly," she insisted, "and I *have* missed you terribly."

"I want to see you before we dock in Rio," he said. "You know what I mean?"

She nodded. "Yes, dear, I know: you want to do my hair."

"Yes," he said. "If those are the only crumbs you can throw my way, I'll take them."

"No, I'm . . . I'm afraid to trust myself that close to you again," she said. "We're both of us much too adult to be having all those preliminaries and no fruition." And then, abruptly, she ran her fingers through her hair. "Unless, of course, my hair looks all that bad. Does it?"

"It's a *mess*, believe me. Please, darling, let me book an appointment for you the first thing in the morning."

"No, Paul, not you. I wouldn't dare. I know, I'll let your friend, Roy, do the honors."

"Roy? Are you insane? Why, he'd have your panties off so fast it'd make your head spin!"

"Oh, surely not, Paul. He's your friend."

"I know, but in a situation like this one he's inclined to be a bit of an opportunist. And besides, now that he knows it can be done, he wouldn't hesitate to try."

"Oh, he *knows*, does he?"

"I didn't have to tell him, if that's what you're thinking. He was wise to what we were doing from that first morning."

"Oh my God, then we're sunk!"

"No, no, we're safe in that department. Roy may be a lot of things, but he's not a fink. Which means I can trust him to keep a secret, but not to keep his hands off you, if you parked yourself in his booth and let him draw the curtain."

"Oh, the hell with my hair," she said. "I'll just put it up in rollers tonight and hope for the best. Now listen, before I dash off, remember we both booked rooms at the Trocadero on Copacabana Beach?"

"Yes, of course. Don't tell me you've changed your mind."

"No, but I just wanted you to know that Andrew has booked a whole suite at the same hotel."

"Well now, isn't that beautiful!"

"No, Paul, these reservations were made long before I ever met him. It's just one of those crazy coincidences. So, when I let it slip where I'd be staying, I had no idea he would be so close. That means he and his friends will be all over that place, in the lobby, the dining room, the pool. So you see, we'll still have to be very careful about letting him and his friends see us being too chummy together."

"But *why*, for God's sake?" he demanded.

"Will you please lower your voice!" she whispered. "The reason, as you might suspect, is that Andrew is very tight with Captain Halprin and his crowd, so if he or his friends ever learn that the ship's cruise director is having it on with one of the resident hairdressers, it could be all over for us in not quite the way we've planned it."

"Okay, so what does that mean? Do I have to go on pretending I don't know you, even when we're ashore in Rio? Oh, honey, that's a great big, luscious paradise we'll be throwing away, don't you realize that?"

"No, it won't be that bad. Andrew is only staying at the hotel for three days. Then he and his party are leaving for Brasilia where they're planning to be house guests for some exiled prince . . ."

"Hmm, a Nazi, no doubt," Paul said. And then: "Hey, wait a minute. Does that mean he won't be sailing back to London?"

"No," she said, smiling. "I was surprised, too, but it seems that was never the plan."

Then he frowned again. "But we have to give up three glorious days in Rio because of him, and that leaves us only two more days remaining. Unless . . ." he suddenly gave her a devilish, naughty-boy grin, "unless we jump ship in Rio and get married there."

She let out a gasp. "Why, Mr. Barrington, sir, how you do sweep a girl off her feet."

"What the hell does that mean, yes or no?"

"It means we have no more time to talk right now," she said, rising. "But at least now you know the score about what to expect in Rio."

"But I don't know the score," he said. "Come back here . . ."

"*Olé, Señor,*" she waved at him over her shoulder. "Meet you at the Trocadero."

The only reply Paul could think of was the one he now muttered under his breath: "Bitch!"

SIXTEEN

Paul's relentless pursuit of Joanna Carroll during the voyage had totally distracted him from the fact that this would be his very first visit to Rio de Janeiro. It seemed incredible that he could have lost sight of something that had always been so important to him. Even as a boy, some of his first dreams of travel had involved sailing down to Rio. For many years, he continued to know very little about this city, and until lately, he'd assumed it was situated at the mouth of the Amazon. Nevertheless, the connotations and reverberations of the very words, "Rio de Janeiro," had remained boundlessly exotic and exciting for him.

Now, at last, he was to find out why.

Early that morning, after being at sea for three long weeks, they drew close to the Tropic of Capricorn and suddenly saw a high, green headland to starboard. This was *Cabo Frio,* or Cold Cape. For days they had been sailing on a southerly bearing, parallel with the coast of Brazil, which for thousands of miles runs approximately north-south. Now they turned to follow an indentation in the coast that starts at *Cabo Frio* and stretches east-west. Rio lies in the middle of this indentation, facing not east towards Africa, as many people imagine, but south towards Antarctica.

All morning they had sailed along that coastline, as schools of dolphins sped out to join them and leap high out of the water from beneath their bows. Paul and Roy had just sat down to lunch when the captain announced over the loudspeaker, "Ladies and gentlemen, we are now approaching Rio."

"Come on, Paul," said Roy, leaping up from the table. "We can eat later. This I've got to see."

For the first time in many weeks, what Paul saw that morning completely erased all thoughts of Joanna Carroll from his mind. Only his first visit to Hong Kong had equaled the excitement he felt that morning as he watched the scattered elements of the view — mountains and forests, ocean and beaches — all resolving themselves into a coherent picture of Rio from the sea. The sun shone between the clouds in celestial beams, and humpbacked islands lay scattered about like a school of resting whales. On top of a tall peak, clearly visible from far out at sea, an immense statue of Christ with outstretched hands appeared and disappeared among the clouds, like something lost in space.

Some 2,000 feet or more below the statue, squeezed between mountains and the sea like plaster of Paris in a mold, lay the city: an unbroken line of brilliant white high-rises whose rectangular façades gleamed in the sun. From such a distance, the city presented a curiously ethereal aspect. No noise emanated from it, no smells, no squalor, no signs of its human inhabitants. Poised nebulously between air and water, Rio seemed a dream city — the most beautiful place in the world.

"Paul, your mouth is hanging open so wide, one of these dolphins is liable to jump in."

Paul nodded, still enraptured. "And to think, this has been down here all this time, and I haven't been."

As the ship drew in closer, the two started identifying places from their map. They were approaching the narrow opening of Guanabara Bay, a huge, balloon-shaped natural harbor on whose western shore the center of the city lies. As they drew level with the bay, they were no more than a quarter of a mile from the land, and the city's humped and angular mountain profile rose before them against the trop-ical sky. They saw the conical form of Sugar Loaf Moun-tain, which stood on the west side of the entrance to the bay. And along the coast to the west was Copacabana, that long ellipse of brilliant white sand that the people of Rio consider a beach without equal.

They moved slowly past the beach as scores of gaping passengers trained their binoculars on the little brown fig-ures that inhabited it. After a rocky headland, they came to the second ellipse of Ipanema and Lebon beaches, with a crust of umbrellas like colored buttons and the ocean coming to an end in a long line of foaming surf.

"Did you ever see anything so spectacular?" Paul said.

"Oh, it's gorgeous," said Roy, "and no mistake. But from what I've read, it isn't all that perfect up close. I hear there's as much ugliness and poverty as there is beauty."

"Yes, but certainly that's no surprise. I can't think of any modern city that doesn't have the same freaky mixtures, the good with the bad, the glamour up against the garbage. Acapulco was a perfect example of that."

Later that day, as Paul, Roy, and Jason were taxiing to their hotel, they did, indeed, find the city to be a fortune of mixed blessings. Although it was late November, the weather was sweltering. And no wonder, since this was the beginning of Rio's summer holiday season. The streets were jammed with pedestrians, buses, and commuter cars. Their driver drove at a suicidal pace which, Paul later heard, was normal for Rio. By the time they made it to their hotel, Paul's dream of Rio as a city of lotus-eaters and infinite romance had grown a little worn at the edges. He knew then that this was a mortal city like any other, inhabited by people preoccupied with the daily realities of the human condition, with living and dying, getting and spending in a world where fate was blind.

Happily, the Hotel Trocadero, across from the Copacabana Beach, was located in one of the city's least squalid areas. Actually, Copacabana and Ipanema, together with the high-rises behind them, constitute what is known as the South Zone, a strip of land along the Atlantic so narrowly compressed between the mountains and the sea that it is only five streets deep at the western end, and only three streets deep at its eastern end. Yet the South Zone contained fully one-sixth of the population of the city, and its high-rise apartments are among the most coveted and expensive living units in the world.

This must be Andrew Steadwell's turf, thought Paul, whenever he decides to hang around long enough. But when he's only here a few days, a simple luxury hotel suite will do nicely. These thoughts brought Joanna back to his mind for the first time that day. Now that it had been two days since they had spoken, Paul wondered if she had been totally honest with him, after all. Did Steadwell only plan to stay in Rio for a few days and move on, or was that just something Joanna had told him to keep him away from the happy couple while they went out on the town together?

Once again, he decided to let Rio fill his mind and his senses for the next few days. After the boys got settled in their rooms, they went out for the lunch they had missed earlier. Their table looked out onto the beach as they, at first, sipped strong black Brazilian coffee, followed by large servings of fresh fruit. Considering the heat of the day, Paul found that an extraordinary vitality filled the city, a restless energy and exuberance. People drifted in an unending stream out of the deep shadows of the side streets into the blinding sunshine of the Avenida Atlantica: bikini-clad young girls tanned to the color of chocolate; millionaires with borzoi dogs; bronzed youths with cut-off jeans; mothers in strapless beachrobes called *tomara-que-caia*, which is Portugese for, "If only it would fall."

Later, Paul and Roy changed into their trunks and went down to the beach, though Jason begged off, saying he had a big hunger to scout out the action. After first soaking their bodies in suntan oil, the other two stretched out on the sand. There was no breeze off the sea that afternoon. Brilliant butterflies from the forested mountains above the city fluttered across the sands, and huge frigate birds with seven-foot wingspans and long tails soared over the penthouse suites of the apartment blocks, circling effortlessly on the thermals above the softening asphalt. After a bit, Roy and Paul rented a beach umbrella, then dozed off under its protection.

When they awoke about an hour later, Roy made a rather incredible announcement. "I've got the most outrageous big erection of my entire career!"

Paul looked at him and burst out laughing. "What's that supposed to be, a news bulletin?"

"No, dummy, it only proves a kind of theory I've got about this place. I think the whole city is like one big blossom of an aphrodisiac. Lord, you can just smell all that raunchy sensuality in the air."

Paul chuckled. "Come off it, Roy, you'd probably say the same thing if you were stranded in Iceland."

"You mean to tell me you don't *feel* it?"

"Yes, I do feel something tropical," said Paul. "But at the moment, it's making me feel more languid than horny. But look, don't let that stop you, Roy. If you want to dash off on your own, fine. I'll check on you later."

As Roy clambered to his feet, he quickly draped his beach towel over his crotch, then gave Paul a sly grin. "Wouldn't do to get mobbed by all these nubile señoritas before I've had time to make a selection."

"So long, Roy," Paul waved him on. "Happy hunting. But please, do try not to catch anything social."

During the next two days, Paul worked on his suntan in the mornings, then joined a group of his co-workers in the afternoons for a series of sightseeing tours, conducting himself as much like a naive, wide-eyed tourist as most of the ship's passengers. In this situation, everyone's behavior was very similar: they gaped in awe and wonder, then made quick grabs for their cameras.

On the second night, Paul had dinner with Jason and Roy, after which they both scooted off on their own separate dates. It was still quite early, only about eight o'clock, so Paul headed for the bar, which adjoined the hotel's main dining room. On his way across the lobby, he happened to run into Laura, the girl he'd almost had a date with earlier that week. He'd almost forgotten what an arresting little beauty she was, with her honey-blonde hair and her petite but voluptuous figure. Since she was alone, and not with one of the ship's officers—nor her sister, for that matter— Paul invited her to join him at the bar for a drink.

She readily accepted, but quickly went into a long apology for her behavior the other night. "You see, Paul, I'm trying to get in as much living as I can during this trip, because the kind of man I'm about to marry back home in Cedar Rapids is the kind of guy who pays very short shrift to anything sexual."

Paul smiled. "Are you saying he's fast in the saddle?"

"Are you kidding?" she said, giggling. "He hardly makes it into the stirrups."

Paul laughed heartily at this. "Well then, my heart goes out to you."

"It's shameful of me to make fun of him, though, the poor darling . . . he does try so hard. But what's a girl to do? I do love him to distraction, you know, and of course he owns most of the downtown section of town. But getting back to that officer. One look at anything in a uniform and

I absolutely melt. Only he passed out before I got a chance, and right in my bed, or do you call it bunk?"

"I call it bad luck."

"Well, anyway, I think I managed to have my way with him, riding him bareback in his sleep, incredibly enough, which is the first time that's ever happened to me. I guess that would make him a somnambulistic fornicator, if there is such a thing. But then, he must have come to in the middle of the night, because when I woke up, he wasn't there. Of course, leave it to my little sister: she made out like gangbusters. She seems to think she's engaged, but I told her she would regret marrying a sailor, don't you agree?"

"If you're talking about the officers I saw you girls with that night, I happen to know they're both married."

"Well, for heaven's sake!" she gaped at him. "Now wouldn't that jar your slats?"

"Indubitably," said Paul, beginning to wonder if this flaky little doxy was as unpredictable in bed as she was in a cocktail lounge. It was with these titillating thoughts in mind that Paul was suddenly struck dumb by something he saw across the room. It was Joanna entering the dining room, not only with Andrew Steadwell, but a whole super-chic group of overdressed plutocrats that included the equally pompous Captain Halprin. They were all in Stead-well's age bracket, which Paul now figured had to be some-where between fifty and death.

Just *look* at that pretentious bastard! he thought, glow-ering and pivoting around on his stool. He so damned tall and rangy and dressed with such effortless expense and bad taste, with that phony mane of platinum-white hair, all frosted and lacquered. Was that Joanna's idea of romance? He looked positively embalmed!

As their party was led to a table, Paul saw a clue he couldn't believe: Joanna and Steadwell were holding hands. Then, as he watched, Steadwell leaned over and kissed her cheek, whereupon she gave him a dazzling smile, then snuggled very cozily close to him.

Infuriated, Paul was suddenly determined to have Joanna see him with Laura. He slipped an arm about the girl's waist and, none too graciously, said, "Come on, let's dance!"

As he pulled her along the floor, he hardly noticed how she struggled to get free of him. "Wait just a minute here!" she said, tugging at him.

"What for? Don't you dance?"

"Are you crazy? I dance like an angel. But you, my friend, seem to have forgotten something."

"Like what?"

"There's no music yet!"

"Oh." Paul glanced at the bandstand where a Latin combo was tuning up for the evening's diversion. "Okay, then let's go into the dining room and have dinner. Would you like that?"

She giggled. "Of course I would have loved it, if only you'd thought to ask me before I'd already had it."

"Oh, certainly . . . yeah, it is rather late, isn't it? For dinner, I mean. I had mine hours ago."

She eyed him quizzically for a moment as they resumed their seats at the bar.

"Mr. Barrington, may I ask you a question?"

"Of course."

"Are you about to throw some kind of a fit or something? Because, honestly, in the past three minutes you have undergone the most amazing series of personality changes. Now, you don't look as if you've been drinking too much, so maybe you've gotten too much sun. Blondes do tend to burn, you know, and while you do look strikingly handsome and rather tasty with your curly hair bleached even lighter by the sun, not to mention the sultry dark tan of your skin . . . well, chances are you might be feeling a little feverish."

"Possible," he said, still glancing in the direction of Joanna and her crowd. "You're sure you don't want to go in there and have dinner anyway, just for the hell of it?"

"No, really, I'm done stuffing my mouth for the day. With food, I mean." She reached over and let her hand rest on his thigh. "But I have another idea. Why don't you come upstairs with me to my suite, and I promise I'll do my level best to cure whatever's ailing you."

Paul gave this some thought, but realized it would be no way to make Joanna jealous, since she wouldn't be able to watch how gymnastically he was making out with another girl. "No, I'm sorry, Laura, that wouldn't do it. I'll have to come up with a much better idea than that."

She glared at him, clearly outraged. "Why, you insulting sonofabitch! You must think you're God's gift to everything female. Well, let me tell you something, to me you're nothing but a . . . a hairdresser. What's more, the man I'm going to marry can afford to buy and sell a whole boatload of ditsy little wage-earners like you!"

With that, she slid off the bar stool and pranced out of the room in a huff.

Rather wistfully, Paul watched her buns swinging angrily in retreat, wondering if all American girls were so spoiled and touchy and, if so, what, then, could he expect from the Canadians, especially when they were young, ambitious, and power-crazed?

With that tragic thought in mind, he decided to get very, very drunk.

SEVENTEEN

Two hours later, after downing prodigious amounts of rum highballs, Paul was feeling no pain. He felt so blissfully anesthetized, he could even say Joanna's name aloud without wanting to grind his teeth. Rum had been the antidote, of course, rum . . . the opiate of the masses. The Steadwell party hadn't yet emerged from the dining room, but Paul had a feeling that if he waited at the bar any longer, he'd be in no condition to keep them under surveillance, which was what he fully intended to do. Once and for all, he wanted solid proof that Joanna had been lying to him about her "platonic" relationship with Steadwell.

Making a superhuman effort not to stagger, he strolled languidly out of the bar, feeling so incongruously jolly, as if he could have danced all night . . . on his hands, if necessary. Oddly enough, he felt morbid and sad and weirdly euphoric, all at once. True, he'd been given his most definitive comeuppance earlier that night, had his total identity handed to him, *en casserole,* so to speak: he was Paul Barrington, ship's hairdresser and rejected clown, the classic kind of victim he always swore he would never be, the guy who trusted the wrong woman, the gal who had done him wrong. Though, first, he meant to prove it, which meant the defendant, Joanna Carroll, was presumed innocent until he actually saw her being guilty.

He sat in the vast lobby, hoping he was being as unobtrusive as any house detective. But he only had to keep that vigil about ten minutes when he saw the culprits emerging from the dining room. Steadwell and Joanna were still arm in arm, and they were laughing, which surely had to be a dead giveaway. They stood there chatting with their friends for a few moments, then bade them goodnight. The others, including Captain Halprin, all headed for the hotel's exit, obviously going on to another nightclub.

Joanna and Steadwell did not join them. Instead, still arm in arm, they headed for the elevators. Of course, that in itself wasn't surprising, since they were both staying at the same hotel. What was surprising, however, was the comparatively early hour: it was only ten-thirty. The night was young in Rio de Janeiro, so, if they were about to turn in, Paul wanted to know where. Which room, in other words; hers or his? And if these two were just pals, beddie-bye was out, right? Wrong, he decided. Pals like these played around. Keeping at a safe distance, he followed them across the lobby.

Earlier, Paul had done a little research that now came in handy. He had checked to find out each of their room numbers. Steadwell's was on the ninth floor, and Joanna's was on the twelfth. All he'd have to do was find out which of their rooms was vacant after they went up and, by the process of elimination, he would know exactly where they were getting it on.

After they got into one of the elevators and the doors closed, Paul scurried quickly across the lobby, his speedy movements winning him considerable attention, even from the worldly Brazilians. He stood before the bank of elevators and studied the board of brightly lit numbers that recorded his enemies' climb upward. A little amazed that he could still count in his bleary-eyed state, he followed the blinkers upwards, three, four, five, six, seven, nine — and it did *not* stop on nine — then ten, eleven, twelve. It stopped on twelve for Joanna.

Paul stared at that light until he started seeing double, but the little bugger never moved! It remained on twelve for what seemed like an eternity. Never went back to the ninth floor, where Andrew should be locked in his room and strapped into his *bed*, that dirty old billionaire, with all his blue-chip dynasties. Just when he began to hope the elevator was stuck, it finally moved. But instead of going back to nine, it went all the way up to twenty-two.

Paul kept staring, until the lights made their next move, down to seventeen, eleven, four, and then bingo! the lobby. The elevator never went back to the ninth floor.

There we have it, ladies and gentlemen of the jury, the evidence we've all been seeking: the two defendants are now in the same room together where they are *not* playing Dominoes! And this time, there was no denying the nature of their involvement. Figures don't lie: he *had* to be in her room, or else the elevator would have shot right down to his floor, the ninth. For immediate confirmation of this, Paul ran swiftly to the lobby phones and dialed Steadwell's room. He let it ring eight times, but there was no answer.

Now he was ready for the *coup de grâce*. With great dispatch and buckling ankles, Paul slithered into the same guilty elevator and pressed button twelve. I'll get to the bottom of this, he thought, as the cage ascended. When he made it to the twelfth floor, he realized he had forgotten her room number. He stood there trying to wrack his brain but the rum of the night had beaten him to it. It seemed so crazy that he had remembered her lover's room number but not hers.

And then it came to him, out of the blue: *1239*. Numerologically speaking, that would spell curtains for both of them. Lady SuperBitch had broken her promise, so now Paul would break Steadwell's jaw. Then he'd plant a few depth charges along his belly, butt, and groin and *ruin* the old dinosaur for confiscating territory that he, Paul, hadn't even begun to plow.

Feeling like one of those cuckolded characters in a French farce, Paul knocked lightly on her door. As he stood there waiting, he felt another clutch of rum-induced vertigo, but managed to shake this off with a great, soaring vigor telling him he was perfectly justified in what he was doing. He would catch this lying maneater in the act of being "platonic" which, according to Joanna's translation, meant that every time she and her Andrew played, it was a tonic.

He heard someone stirring inside. Voices, plural, and he was certain it was a man's and a woman's, lewdly interwoven. He tried to make it down to the keyhole but got so dizzy, the floor came up and hugged him for a minute. He sat there and ruminated for a few seconds, recouping his militancy, not to mention his wits. Then up like an arrow again, deciding he didn't need any keyhole previews to pave the way.

He knocked again. This time the voices stopped.

"Yes? Who is it, please?" Joanna.

"It is I, Paul Barrington, boy imbecile," he said, with the timbre of a house detective. "Let me in, or I'll . . ." He was about to say 'I'll huff and I'll puff,' but he didn't have the wind.

She unlocked the door and pulled it open, though only slightly. She was wearing a very filmy-looking peignoir, and how it clung. Paul had never seen her in anything that abbreviated before, not even in his lap while he was almost doing her hair. Naturally, the garment made her look appropriately depraved, under the circumstances. All the trimmings of a gold-digger's seduction, right there on her back. Paul stood on his toes, trying to spot Randy Andy over her shoulder. Probably under the bed, he thought; he's too big to hang from the chandelier.

"Paul, what on earth?" she said. Then she turned up her nose as she smelled the rum fumes. "Good heavens, you're drunk, aren't you?" Then she laughed. What gall of the woman! To stand right there in her doorway and laugh at him. Talk about twisting the knife! "I think that's cute," she said. "Until now, I think I've seen you in every mood except gassed. Oh well, I suppose you deserve your share of relaxation. But listen, dear, it's getting late, so hadn't you best trot off to bed?"

"I'll trot off to bullshit!" he announced. Then he pushed his way into her room. "Ah hah!" he exclaimed. "You see what a tangled web we weave when first we practice to . . . where the hell *is* he . . . ?"

"Where is who, for heaven's sake?" she said, softly closing the door behind him.

It was so dark in her room compared to the brightly lit hallway, Paul went blind for a minute. Then he zoomed downward to peer under her bed and suffered another attack of rum vertigo. The room spun around his head like a carousel, until suddenly, there he was, on the floor again, like some silly little kid who'd been thrown from his rockinghorse. Joanna switched on the glaring overhead light. Paul quickly peeked under her bed again, nearly having to stand on his head to do it (pretty low bed). And what do you know, Andrew wasn't there. The guy sure moved fast for his age.

Paul heard someone laughing, and when he looked up, he saw Joanna standing over him. She was practically helpless with hilarity, clutching all that flowing female gear about her luscious bosom, her lovely russet hair falling about her shoulders. It was indecent of her to be dressed like that when she was entertaining, though come to think of it, dressed like that she was more entertaining than he'd ever seen her. But not for *me*, he thought. "Where'd he go, out on the veranda?"

This brought on another mirthful seizure from her, until the tears rolled down her cheeks. Wow, he thought, I must be a riot. "Oh, Paul, I'm so sorry," she said, dabbing at her eyes with a hankie, "but you really are too much. If you could just see yourself. It's all very charming and silly, of course, and we must do it again sometime, when the two of us can start out even. Of course, if you still insist on playing the game, I want you to feel perfectly free to search the closet, then the bathroom. But darling, I assure you, Andrew Steadwell is not, nor has he ever been in this room. If only you were sober enough to tell me what made you so sure he *was* . . ."

Saying nothing, he made it to his feet and made a dash for the closet. He pulled open the door. "Okay, Mr. Industrial Waste, I know you're a lot older than I am, so if you come out of there like a gentleman, I promise to let you take the first swing. Then, old man, I shall throw you right out the window." He was so proud of that speech, he almost cried when he saw Steadwell wasn't in the closet, or the bathroom either.

Then he turned and gaped stupidly at his ravishing half-dressed tormentor. And it suddenly dawned on him: I'm all alone with her in her bedroom, and she's got nothing on underneath that gossamer hunk of whatever it is that's revealing everything I've never had enough of.

"Wait a minute, Joanna, I heard voices in here. I know I did."

She pointed to a small, portable radio on her nightstand. "Radio Free Europe, Paul. I'm never without it."

"Oh, my God!" he muttered lamely, staring at the instrument. "And that's such a worthy cause, too. I mean, who'll ever forget Tokyo Rose . . .?" Then he remembered his real evidence, the elevators. "Now dammit, your elevator stopped on twelve and never budged, not until it shot up to twenty-two. But Andrew's on nine, so explain that, if you can."

"I really think that's the first accurate statement you've made since you barged in here. Andrew's room *is* on the ninth floor, and that's precisely where he is right now, I would imagine. And after what you said about the elevators, I would also assume that after seeing me to *my* door — without coming in, mind you — he waited on this floor for the elevator, but when it took too long in coming, he must have walked down the three flights to his own floor."

"He *walked* down?" Paul gaped at her as if this was the most outrageous development of the whole evening. "And after I nearly went blind, staring at those bloody blinkers, he had the unmitigated gall to *walk* down?" Then he thought of something else. "No, wait a minute. I immediately phoned his room and there was no answer."

She smiled. "The key word there, dear, is 'immediately.' Obviously, he hadn't yet reached his room, not if he first waited for the elevator, and then walked down."

Paul stood there for a moment, trying to hold onto his anger, but when he realized exactly what must have happened, he finally let it slip away. And now, he also succumbed to fits of laughter, full of such unbridled joy and relief, because look: Andrew wasn't here and hadn't *been* here. Well, at least not tonight.

Now he couldn't take his eyes off her, standing there like that, with the door closed and nobody around to spy on them or report them. He wanted her so much in that moment, it almost sobered him up, just to look at her in that gorgeous see-through whatever it was that revealed all those taunting contours of hips and breasts like a Degas figurine come to life. It wasn't only that he was about to climb the walls from a case of terminal celibacy. No, he was in love with her, but more than that: he was obsessed with the way it made him feel to know it.

"Okay, then it wasn't what it seemed, with you and Andrew. Even though you two have spent an awful lot of time together since we arrived in Rio."

"Well, there *is* an explanation for that, Paul, something I haven't had time to tell you. Actually, I didn't find out about it until the day before we docked."

"Find out what?"

"By the sheerest coincidence, I found out that Andrew and my father knew each other during the war. Isn't that fantastic?"

"Steadwell was a soldier?" he said. "On whose side?"

"Now come on, Paul, I'm being serious! It seems they both served as lieutenant commanders in the Pacific. Andrew had some marvelous stories to tell me about their years in service together. You see, we've never been able to get Dad to talk about his navy experiences, even though he was decorated several times over. So you can see why it meant a lot to me to hear it all firsthand from one of his buddies . . ."

Paul said nothing for a moment, letting this new information wash over him. It certainly put everything on another level: friend of the family instead of a rival? Do I buy this? he asked himself. Oh hell, I think I'd better. I'm getting so tired of shopping around for something I can really believe about this woman.

"Well now, in the war together, eh?" he said, and knew he was grinning at her like a village idiot in his eagerness to believe her. "So it's really been more like old home week for you than a mad escapade."

"Yes, it's been a real comfort for both of us. You see, despite all his money, Andrew happens to be very troubled right now. He doesn't show it, of course."

"No; you've got that right."

"He's terribly in love with the wife who recently divorced him and he wants her back. That's why he's taking this trip, to give himself time to think. So he talked to me a great deal about this problem, and I think it helped him."

"But, I saw you two holding hands and . . . and laughing, and well, looking very affectionate."

"Oh, that's just how he is around women, being gallant, attentive, the charming escort. Believe me, no matter how

it may have looked to you, for me there was nothing signif-
icant going on, nothing intimate nor even very personal."
Then suddenly her voice broke and she looked as if she were
about to cry. "Oh, damn you, Paul, I'm so in love with you
and it's been so ghastly, not being able to do enough about
it, so please don't make things worse by these awful doubts
of yours . . ."

Paul heard the invitation in her voice, so he knew the
time for standing on ceremony had at last come to an end.
With one forward leap, he had her in his arms and held
her for a long, engulfing kiss, keeping his mouth on hers so
she would have no more chance to speak either lies or truths;
he wanted only the pantomime of their feelings to be his
final proof. He let his hands roam all over her body, refusing to end the kiss, thinking this was the one towering
moment when he would know if she had been lying about
Andrew, if he'd been something more than an old war
buddy of her father's. And then, after a moment, he felt
the kind of tremors and responses from her that didn't know
how to lie, felt the power and the tumult of what it was
doing to her to feel him so close to her.

"No, wait, darling," she said. "Should we really let it
happen like this, tonight, when you've had so much to
drink?"

"You know I'm sober now, Joanna. Surely you can feel
how sober I've become in just these last few moments." He
drew her close again and she didn't struggle, and he was
kissing her again and tasting the soft warm textures of her
skin, their sighs blending as she pressed against him and
moaned, the two of them swaying there a little, clinging.
He held her at arm's length for a moment and he saw the
soft beam of recognition in her eyes that told him she
wanted everything he did. She stepped back, smiled, and
with movements of purest grace, she removed her robe. As
he had suspected, there was nothing underneath to bar their

way, no more silly barriers to keep them waiting in the wings.

He stared at her. She was incredibly beautiful. He tried to tell her so. "Oh, Joanna, look at you. Right now, I want . . . I want . . ."

". . . Please, darling, don't tell me you want to do my hair . . ."

Then he said no more and reached for her, and began touching her, very carefully and everywhere, his fingers fluttering like homing pigeons to all those soft and tender places, hands toying and acquainting, hands full of celebration.

They spent only a few hours together that night. Before dawn, Paul sped down the back stairs to his own room, if only to preserve what little was left of their floating careers. Those hours together had confirmed what had only been a dreamy suspicion until now. What they had felt for one another was as they had known it would be, a fusion that grew lovelier and more varied with each new moment they touched. In short, they were very good together, so Paul decided it was time to forget all past doubts, time to rejoice.

And yet, even while he slept in his own room later that night, there was an underlying current of doubt that continued to nag at him. He felt a vague uneasiness about her father and Steadwell being old war buddies, but the force of everything else he was feeling for her managed to obscure those anxieties. After sleeping only a few hours, he awoke wanting her again. It was only six-thirty a.m. He got up, hurriedly dressed, and crept back upstairs to her room.

"You mad, adorable lunatic!" she said, when she saw him standing in the hallway. "I wanted you to appear, and here you are. Come on, don't stand there, wasting precious time . . . !" And this time she initiated everything they set in motion. They had a delicious, long encore in bed which further displaced those lingering suspicions from his mind. Overnight, she had become like a whole new addiction for him. The thought that he might never be able to get enough of her had him feeling both worried and excited all at once. It was then that they made their plans, though little did Paul know how quickly they would be subject to change. "In Londontown, we will marry," she said between kisses, "and somehow we'll manage to be secretly engaged all during the return voyage."

"Secrets again," he said. "I'm sick to death of secrets. Why can't I have you in the main ballroom, like everyone else?"

"You fiend, I'll get you for that," she said, reaching for more of him. "Down here," she said, scooping, treasuring, "and here . . . oh, and especially there . . . !"

What a wonder girl, he thought, what a prize. And so limber, too.

Later that day, they were having lunch in the hotel dining room with a few fellow workers from the ship, including Jason and Roy and two young Rio tigresses the boys had adopted who, comfortably enough, could speak no English. By now it had become common knowledge that Paul and Joanna were something of an item, even though neither of them had told anyone they were officially engaged.

At one point, Joanna got up to go to the ladies' room. As she walked across the restaurant, she encountered Andrew Steadwell and Captain Halprin as they made their entrance.

Curious, Paul watched as they chatted for a few moments. Then, much to his surprise, Joanna smiled and pointed across the room directly at him. Both Steadwell and the captain glanced Paul's way, and they also smiled. Then they continued chatting for another few minutes, until Joanna made her exit to the ladies' room. At the same time, both the captain and Steadwell made a beeline for Paul.

Good God, he thought, what is she up to now?

"Barrington, my friend," said the captain. "Let me be the first to congratulate you on your engagement."

Paul felt everybody's eyes fastened on him as he rose, smiled, and tried to look nonchalant.

"You're certainly getting a wonderful girl in Miss Carroll," Halprin was saying. "What's more, I thoroughly approve of your plan to have me perform the wedding ceremony at sea . . ."

"Hey, Paul!" said Jason. "You sneaky devil!"

"What were you going to do, wait 'til the last minute to let *us* in on your little secret?" demanded Roy.

"Actually, I consider it an honor," the captain said. "We'll do the whole thing in the main ballroom. I'm sure it will serve as an added festivity for the passengers, and so very romantic, too, especially with such a handsome young couple. Yes, I think it's a really marvelous idea!"

"Yes, marvelous," Paul muttered. Jesus, he thought, this girl was full of surprises. They hadn't even given their notice to resign yet, and here she was, planning a floating three-ring circus for their wedding.

The captain quickly introduced Paul and his friends to Andrew Steadwell.

"Barrington manages our gift shop and beauty salon," Halprin explained, "and we shall certainly hate to lose him after the ship docks in London. And Miss Carroll, too. Just about everybody had a crush on that girl."

"And you can certainly add me to that list," said Steadwell. "That is one remarkable lady you're getting there, Mr. Barrington. And frankly, I don't mind telling you I wish I had been more her type. But what the hell, that's the way the libido crumbles, and I guess it's not always the best man who wins." He followed this slur with a hearty laugh.

Although Paul kept smiling, his ears kept doing a playback of Steadwell's phrase: "I wish I had been more her type."

Why would he wish that if he were such an old friend of her father's? Wasn't that incest?

Then Paul made a stab at it. "Talking about the war, Mr. Steadwell," he blurted out, although nobody had been. "Aren't you glad it's been over with these past eleven years?"

Steadwell stared blankly at him for a moment. Then he laughed, this time with amusement. "What war was that? Hell, I was too old for the Koreans and 4F for the Japs and the Heinies. I've got a trick knee, worse luck. But, what're you gonna do?"

As Paul stood there, watching the men go over to a table of their own, it was suddenly clear to him what had been bothering him about Joanna's story. Her father was a British Canadian, so he would not have served with anyone in the U.S. Navy. If anything, the RAF would be more like it.

But, by the time he resumed his seat, Paul was inwardly laughing at the sweet, sexy irony of it all. Okay, so Joanna wasn't perfect, after all. But one thing was for certain: she was *his* bundle of imperfections, nobody else's. And since it was clear from what Steadwell had said that she really hadn't given him a tumble, Paul was further convinced she had devised these little plots and intrigues only because she so enjoyed watching the effect it had on him, even got some erotic kind of thrill to see him "disturbed" and all riled up. Apparently, these were the games she wanted to play with him and, as he saw it, this, too, was part of the way she desired him.

When she returned to the table, she pretended to be surprised that Paul and the others were talking about the big "superstar glamour wedding" to be held on board the ship.

"My goodness," she said as she slid into the seat next to him, "good news sure travels fast."

He slipped an arm about her waist and whispered, "Bitch. Must the husband always be the last to know?"

"Paul, so help me God, that idea never even occurred to me until I saw the captain here this morning. And then, suddenly, it all fell into place, and it seemed so ideal. Remember, you did say you wanted to have me in the main ballroom, like everyone else, but we've also got to look on the practical side. Now we won't have to be secretly engaged during the trip home, *and* we can be married and have our honeymoon, all expenses paid, which means it'll be a working honeymoon, of course, but . . . well, what do you think of that?"

"I think I shall have to watch you very closely from now on . . ."

. . . Which, in one variation or another, was precisely what Paul Barrington did for the next twenty-five years or so. He watched Joanna, in countries all over the world, as well as in planes and ships and trains and shops and salons, and even in childbirth.

Without her adroit and manipulative talents for socializing, Paul might never have achieved his international fame as one of the world's premier hairstylists.

Over the years, he learned to have an amused tolerance for Joanna's gifts of drama and deception, even when he discovered the truth about her father. Due to chronic asthma, the old guy never did see action in any war. But most of all, Paul learned to believe the little white lies she told that were designed only to get a rise out of him. He did so love the way she adored seeing him disturbed.

As for their further adventures on the high seas, the Barringtons never lost their hunger to see a little bit more of the world every year. Never again would they sail the oceans as crew members, however. Those days were gone forever. Gone but, of course, not forgotten since they each, in each other, had a living souvenir on hand to help them remember.

Certainly, Paul could never forget those five lost years in the Fifties, when the world was such a simple place to have fun in. When neither terrorism nor jet travel had yet been invented; when there was so much innocence and laughter, and the sort of sweet, playful silliness you never had to be sorry for later.

It might never happen quite like that for anyone else again, but it happened for Paul Barrington and he remembered it all.

KENNETH PEARCE, better known as Kenneth of London, began his apprenticeship as a hairdresser in London at the age of 14. From 1951–1956 he toured the world aboard luxury liners as a hairstylist and shop manager, logging over 250,000 miles at sea. Pearce has achieved international recognition as a hairstylist. He has opened salons in Europe, the United States, and the Orient. He has appeared frequently on radio and television, and pioneered the use of video training films in the beauty industry. In 1970, Pearce, his wife and two sons moved from London to California. MAKING WAVES is his first novel.